The Most Good You Can Do

THE MOST GOOD YOU CAN DO

HOW EFFECTIVE ALTRUISM IS CHANGING IDEAS ABOUT LIVING ETHICALLY

PETER SINGER

Yale
UNIVERSITY PRESS

New Haven and London

The Castle Lectures in Ethics, Politics, and Economics

Published with assistance from the foundation established in memory of
James Wesley Cooper of the Class of 1865, Yale College.

Yale University Press books may be purchased in quantity for
educational, business, or promotional use. For information, please e-mail
sales.press@yale.edu (U.S. office) or sales@yaleup.co.uk (U.K. office).

Set in Gotham and Adobe Garamond types by IDS Infotech Ltd.
Printed in the United States of America.

Library of Congress Cataloging-in-Publication Data
Singer, Peter, 1946–
The most good you can do: how effective altruism is changing ideas
about living ethically / Peter Singer.
pages cm. — (Castle lectures in ethics, politics, and economics)
Includes bibliographical references and index.
ISBN 978-0-300-18027-5 (cloth : alk. paper) 1. Altruism.
2. Ethics. I. Title.
BJ1474.S56 2015
171'.8—dc23
2014035965

A catalogue record for this book is available from the British Library.

This paper meets the requirements of ANSI/NISO Z39.48–1992
(Permanence of Paper).

10 9 8 7 6 5 4 3 2

Contents

Preface

An exciting new movement is emerging: effective altruism. Student organizations are forming around it, and there are lively discussions on social media pages and websites as well as in the pages of the *New York Times* and the *Washington Post*.

Effective altruism is based on a very simple idea: we should do the most good we can. Obeying the usual rules about not stealing, cheating, hurting, and killing is not enough, or at least not enough for those of us who have the great good fortune to live in material comfort, who can feed, house, and clothe ourselves and our families and still have money or time to spare. Living a minimally acceptable ethical life involves using a substantial part of our spare resources to make the world a better place. Living a fully ethical life involves doing the most good we can.

Although the people most active in the effective altruism movement tend to be millennials—that is, the first generation to have come of age in the new millennium—older philosophers, of whom I am one, have been discussing effective altruism from before it had a name or was a movement. The branch of philosophy known as practical ethics has played an important role in effective altruism's development, and effective altruism in turn vindicates the importance of philosophy, showing that it changes, sometimes quite dramatically, the lives of those who take courses in it.

Most effective altruists are not saints but ordinary people like you and me, so very few effective altruists claim to live a fully ethical life. Most of them are somewhere on the continuum between a minimally acceptable ethical life and a fully ethical life. That doesn't mean that they are constantly feeling guilty about not being morally perfect. Effective altruists don't see a lot of point in feeling guilty. They prefer to focus on the good they are doing. Some of them are content to know they are doing something significant to make the world a better place. Many of them like to challenge themselves, to do a little better this year than last year.

Effective altruism is notable from several perspectives, each of which I will explore in the following pages. First, and most important, it is making a difference to the world. Philanthropy is a very large industry. In the United States alone there are almost one million charities, receiving a total of approximately $200 billion a year with an additional $100 billion donated to religious congregations. A small number of the charities are outright frauds, but a much bigger problem is that very few of them are sufficiently transparent to allow donors to judge whether they are really doing good. Most of that $300 billion is given on the basis of emotional responses to images of the people, animals, or forests that the charity is helping. Effective altruism seeks to change that by providing incentives for charities to demonstrate their effectiveness. Already the movement is directing millions of dollars to charities that are effectively reducing the suffering and death caused by extreme poverty.

Second, effective altruism is a way of giving meaning to our own lives and finding fulfillment in what we do. Many effective altruists say that in doing good, they feel good. Effective altruists directly benefit others, but indirectly they often benefit themselves.

Third, effective altruism sheds new light on an old philosophical and psychological question: Are we fundamentally driven by our innate needs and emotional responses, with our rational capacities doing little more than laying a justificatory veneer over actions that were already determined before we even started reasoning about what to do? Or can reason play a crucial role in determining how we live? What is it that drives some of us to look beyond our own interests and the interests of those we love to the interests of strangers, future generations, and animals?

Finally, the emergence of effective altruism and the evident enthusiasm and intelligence with which many millennials at the outset of their careers are embracing it offer grounds for optimism about our future. There has long been skepticism about whether people can really be motivated by an altruistic concern for others. Some have thought that our moral capacities are limited to helping our kin, those with whom we are, or could be, in mutually beneficial relationships, and members of our own tribal group or small-scale society. Effective altruism provides evidence that this is not the case. It shows that we can expand our moral horizons, reach decisions based on a broad form of altruism, and employ our reason to assess evidence about the likely consequences of our actions. In this way it allows us to hope that the coming generation, and those that follow it, will be able to meet the ethical responsibilities of a new era in which our problems will be global as well as local.

Acknowledgments

The inspiration for this book has come from all who practice effective altruism—you are living refutations of the cynics who say that human beings are just not capable of living as if the well-being of strangers really matters. Your blend of concern for others and a commitment to act on the basis of reason and evidence has built the movement that is at the core of this book. I thank those of you mentioned in the book for allowing me to share your stories with a wider audience. In doing this, you are again following the evidence—in this case, research showing that people are more likely to help strangers when they know that others are doing the same.

My immediate stimulus for taking up this topic was an invitation to give the Castle Lectures at Yale University. I am grateful to the Castle Lectures committee, chaired by Nicholas Sambanis, and to John Castle, who endowed the lectures. There is, as Mr. Castle pointed out over a post-lecture dinner, some tension between my views about donating to very wealthy universities and the fact that his endowment enabled me to present my arguments to hundreds of Yale undergraduates (and now, he could add, to a much wider audience) and thereby to influence their future actions. I very much hope that his gift will do more good than anything else he could have done with that amount of money, although I persist in thinking that, at the time he made it, he could not reasonably have predicted so fortunate an outcome.

Many people have read drafts of the book, or parts of it, and offered helpful comments or responded to my queries. I want to thank, in particular, Anthony Appiah, Paul Bloom, Jon Bockman and Allison Smith for Animal Charity Evaluators, Paul van den Bosch for Give A Kidney, Nick Bostrom, Richard Butler-Bowdon, Di Franks for Living Kidney Donation, Holden Karnofsky for GiveWell, Katarzyna de Lazari-Radek, Peter Hurford, Michael Liffman, Will MacAskill, Yaw Nyarko, Caleb Ontiveros, Toby Ord, Theron Pummer, Rob Reich, Susanne Roff, Agata Sagan, and Aleksandra Taranow. Special thanks to Mona Fixdal, whose splendid assistance in the preparation of my online course "Practical Ethics" made it possible for me to devote more time to writing this book. Figures 1 and 2 are reprinted with the permission of Julia Wise; these illustrations were prepared by Bill Nelson. Finally, I thank the team at Yale University Press: Bill Frucht, my editor, for his constructive criticism throughout the process of writing the book; Lawrence Kenney, for his suggestions at the copyediting stage, Jaya Chatterjee, the assistant editor, and Margaret Otzel, the in-house production editor, for overseeing the production process.

Some passages in the book draw on previously published work. I first wrote about "Batkid" in "Heartwarming causes are nice, but let's give to charity with our heads," *Washington Post*, December 20, 2013. Elements of my argument in chapter 11 appeared in "Good Charity, Bad Charity," *New York Times*, August 11, 2013. Chapter 15 includes material that was previously published in "Preventing Human Extinction," coauthored with Nick Beckstead and Matt Wage and available at: www.effective-altruism.com/preventing-human-extinction. A fuller statement of the argument about the roles of reason and emotion in motivating altruism can be found in chapter 2 of Katarzyna de Lazari-Radek and Peter Singer, *The Point of View of the Universe* (Oxford: Oxford University Press, 2014).

Peter Singer

University Center for Human Values,
Princeton University
&
School of Historical and Philosophical Studies,
University of Melbourne

PART ONE

EFFECTIVE ALTRUISM

1

What Is Effective Altruism?

I met Matt Wage in 2009 when he took my Practical Ethics class at Princeton University. In the readings relating to global poverty and what we ought to be doing about it, he found an estimate of how much it costs to save the life of one of the millions of children who die each year from diseases that we can prevent or cure. This led Matt to calculate how many lives he could save, over his lifetime, assuming that he earned an average income and donated 10 percent of it to a highly effective organization, for example, one providing families with bednets to prevent malaria, a major killer of children. He discovered that he could, with that level of donation, save about one hundred lives. He thought to himself, "Suppose you see a burning building, and you run through the flames and kick a door open, and let one hundred people out. That would be the greatest moment in your life. And I could do as much good as that!"[1]

Two years later Matt graduated. His senior thesis received the Philosophy Department's prize for the best thesis of the year. He was accepted by the University of Oxford for postgraduate study. Many students who major in philosophy dream of an opportunity like that—I know I did—but by then Matt had done a lot of thinking about and discussing with others what career would do the most good. This led him to a very different choice: he took a job on Wall Street, working for an arbitrage trading firm. On a higher income, he would be able to give much more, both as a percentage and in dollars, than 10 percent of a professor's income. One year after graduating, Matt was donating a six-figure sum—roughly half his annual earnings—to highly effective charities. He was on the way to saving a hundred lives, not over his entire career but within the first year or two of his working life and every year thereafter.

Matt is an effective altruist. His choice of career is one of several possible ways of being an effective altruist. Effective altruists do things like the following:

- Living modestly and donating a large part of their income—often much more than the traditional tenth, or tithe—to the most effective charities;
- Researching and discussing with others which charities are the most effective or drawing on research done by other independent evaluators;
- Choosing the career in which they can earn most, not in order to be able to live affluently but so that they can do more good;
- Talking to others, in person or online, about giving, so that the idea of effective altruism will spread;
- Giving part of their body—blood, bone marrow, or even a kidney—to a stranger.

In the following chapters, we will meet people who have done these things.

What unites all these acts under the banner of effective altruism? The definition now becoming standard is "a philosophy and social movement which applies evidence and reason to working out the most effective ways to improve the world."² That definition says nothing about motives or about any sacrifice or cost to the effective altruist. Given that the movement has altruism as part of its name, these omissions may seem odd. Altruism is contrasted with egoism, which is concern only for oneself, but we should not think of effective altruism as requiring self-sacrifice, in the sense of something necessarily contrary to one's own interests. If doing the most you can for others means that you are also flourishing, then that is the best possible outcome for everyone. As we shall see in chapter 9, many effective altruists deny that what they are doing is a sacrifice. Nevertheless they are altruists because their overriding concern is to do the most good they can. The fact that they find fulfillment and personal happiness in doing that does not detract from their altruism.

Psychologists who study giving behavior have noticed that some people give substantial amounts to one or two charities, while others give small amounts to many charities. Those who donate to one or two charities seek evidence about what the charity is doing and whether it is really having a positive impact. If the evidence indicates that the charity is really helping others, they make a substantial donation. Those who give small amounts to many charities are not so interested in whether what they are doing helps others—psychologists call them warm glow givers. Knowing that they are giving makes them feel good, regardless of the impact of their donation. In many cases the donation is so small—$10 or less—that if they stopped to think, they would realize that the cost of processing the donation is likely to exceed any benefit it brings to the charity.³

In 2013, as the Christmas giving season approached, twenty thousand people gathered in San Francisco to watch a five-year-old boy dressed as Batkid ride around the city in a Batmobile with an actor dressed as Batman by his side. The pair rescued a damsel in distress and captured the Riddler, for which they received the keys of "Gotham City" from the mayor—not an actor, he really was the mayor of San Francisco—for their role in fighting crime. The boy, Miles Scott, had been through three years of chemotherapy for leukemia, and when asked for his greatest wish, he replied, "To be Batkid." The Make-A-Wish Foundation had made his wish come true.

Does that give you a warm glow? It gives me one, even though I know there is another side to this feel-good story. Make-A-Wish would not say how much it cost to fulfill Miles's wish, but it did say that the average cost of making a child's wish come true is $7,500.[4] Effective altruists would, like anyone else, feel emotionally drawn toward making the wishes of sick children come true, but they would also know that $7,500 could, by protecting families from malaria, save the lives of at least three children and maybe many more. Saving a child's life has to be better than fulfilling a child's wish to be Batkid. If Miles's parents had been offered that choice—Batkid for a day or a complete cure for their son's leukemia—they surely would have chosen the cure. When more than one child's life can be saved, the choice is even clearer. Why then do so many people give to Make-A-Wish, when they could do more good by donating to the Against Malaria Foundation, which is a highly effective provider of bednets to families in malaria-prone regions? The answer lies in part in the emotional pull of knowing that you are helping *this* child, one whose face you can see on television, rather than the unknown and unknowable children who would have died from malaria if your donation had not provided the nets under which they sleep. It also lies in part in the fact that Make-A-Wish appeals to Americans, and Miles is an American child.

Effective altruists will feel the pull of helping an identifiable child from their own nation, region, or ethnic group but will then ask themselves if that is the best thing to do. They know that saving a life is better than making a wish come true and that saving three lives is better than saving one. So they don't give to whatever cause tugs most strongly at their heartstrings. They give to the cause that will do the most good, given the abilities, time, and money they have available.

Doing the most good is a vague idea that raises many questions. Here are a few of the more obvious ones, and some preliminary answers:

What counts as "the most good"?

Effective altruists will not all give the same answer to this question, but they do share some values. They would all agree that a world with less suffering and more happiness in it is, other things being equal, better than one with more suffering and less happiness. Most would say that a world in which people live longer is, other things being equal, better than one in which people live shorter lives. These values explain why helping people in extreme poverty is a popular cause among effective altruists. As we shall see in more detail in chapter 10, a given sum of money does much more to reduce suffering and save lives if we use it to assist people living in extreme poverty in developing countries than it would do if we gave it to most other charitable causes.

Does everyone's suffering count equally?

Effective altruists do not discount suffering because it occurs far away or in another country or afflicts people of a different race or religion. They agree that the suffering of animals counts too and generally agree that we should not give less consideration to suffering just because the victim is not a member of our species. They may differ, however, on how to weigh the type of suffering animals can experience against the type of suffering humans can experience.[5]

Does "the most good you can do" mean that it is wrong to give priority to one's own children? Surely it can't be wrong to put the interests of members of the family and close friends ahead of the interests of strangers?

Effective altruists can accept that one's own children are a special responsibility, ahead of the children of strangers. There are various possible grounds for this. Most parents love their children, and it would be unrealistic to require parents to be impartial between their own children and other children. Nor would we want to discourage such bias because children thrive in close, loving families, and it is not possible to love people without having greater concern for their well-being than one has for others. In any case, while doing the most good is an important part of the life of every effective altruist, effective altruists are real people, not saints, and they don't seek to maximize the good in every single thing they do, 24/7. As we shall see, typical effective altruists leave themselves time and resources to relax and do what they want. For most of us, being close to our children and other family members or friends is central to how we want to spend our time. Nonetheless, effective altruists recognize that there are limits to how much they should do for their children, given the greater needs of others. Effective altruists do not think their children need all the latest toys or lavish birthday parties, and they reject the widespread assumption that parents should, on their death, leave virtually everything they own to their children rather than give a substantial part of their wealth to those who can benefit much more from it.

What about other values, like justice, freedom, equality, and knowledge?

Most effective altruists think that other values are good because they are essential for the building of communities in which people can live better lives, lives free of oppression, and have greater self-respect and freedom to do what they want as well as experience less suffering and premature death.[6] No doubt some effective altruists hold that these values are also good for their own sake, independently of these consequences, but others do not.

Can promoting the arts be part of "the most good you can do"?

In a world that had overcome extreme poverty and other major problems that face us now, promoting the arts would be a worthy goal. In the world in which we live, however, for reasons that will be explored in chapter 11, donating to opera houses and museums isn't likely to be doing the most good you can.

How many effective altruists could there be? Can everyone practice effective altruism?

It's possible for everyone who has some spare time or money to practice effective altruism. Unfortunately, most people—even, as we shall see in chapter 11, professional philanthropy advisors—don't believe in thinking too much about the choice of causes to support. So it isn't likely everyone will become an effective altruist anytime soon. The more interesting question is whether effective altruists can become numerous enough to influence the giving culture of affluent nations. There are some promising signs that that may be starting to happen.

What if one's act reduces suffering, but to do so one must lie or harm an innocent person?

In general, effective altruists recognize that breaking moral rules against killing or seriously harming an innocent person will almost always have worse consequences than following these rules. Even thoroughgoing utilitarians, who judge actions to be right or wrong entirely on the basis of their consequences, are wary of speculative reasoning that suggests we should violate basic human rights today for the sake of some distant future good. They know that under Lenin, Stalin, Mao, and Pol Pot, a vision of a utopian future society was used to justify unspeakable atrocities, and even today some terrorists justify their crimes by imagining they will bring about a better future. No effective altruist wants to repeat those tragedies.

Suppose I set up a factory in a developing country, paying wages that are better than local workers would otherwise earn and enough to lift them out of extreme poverty. Does that make me an effective altruist, even if I make a profit from the factory?

What are you going to do with your profits? If you decided to manufacture in the developing country in order to make it possible for people to escape extreme poverty, you will reinvest a substantial part of your profits in ways that help more people escape extreme poverty. Then you are an effective altruist. If, on the other hand, you use your profits to live as luxuriously as you can, the fact that you have benefited some of the poor is not sufficient to make you an effective altruist. There are all kinds of intermediate positions between these two extremes. Reinvesting some of your profits to help more people earn a decent income, while retaining enough to live at a much better level than your employees, puts you somewhere on the spectrum of effective altruism—you are living at least a minimally decent ethical life, even if not a perfect one.

What about giving to your college or university? You teach at Princeton University, and this book is based on lectures you gave at Yale University, thanks to the generous gift of a Yale alumnus. Do you deny that giving to such institutions counts as effective altruism?

I count myself fortunate to be teaching at one of the finest educational institutions in the world. This gives me the opportunity to teach very bright, hardworking students like Matt Wage, who are likely to have a disproportionately large influence on the world. For the same reason, I was pleased to accept the invitation to give the Castle Lectures at Yale. But Princeton has an endowment, at the time of writing, of $21 billion, and Yale's is $23.9 billion. At the moment there are enough alumni donating to these universities to ensure that they will continue to be outstanding educational institutions, and the money you donate to one of them could probably do more good elsewhere. If effective altruism ever becomes so popular that these educational institutions are no longer able to do important research at a high level, it will be time to consider whether donating to them might once again be an effective form of altruism.[7]

2

A Movement Emerges

Effective altruism is an offspring with many parents. I can claim to be one of them because in 1972, when I was a junior lecturer at University College, Oxford, I wrote an article called "Famine, Affluence and Morality" in which I argued that, given the great suffering that occurs during famines and similar disasters, we ought to give large proportions of our income to disaster relief funds. How much? There is no logical stopping place, I suggested, until we reach the point of marginal utility—that is, the point at which by giving more, one would cause oneself and one's family to lose as much as the recipients of one's aid would gain. Over the next forty plus years, the essay has been widely reprinted and used by professors around the world to challenge their students' beliefs that they are living ethically.[1]

Here's the rub: even though I argued that this is what we ought to do, I did not do it myself. When I wrote the article, my wife and I were giving away about 10 percent of our modest income (she was working as a high school teacher, earning a little more than I was). That percentage increased over the years. We are now giving away about one-third of what we earn and aiming to get to half, but that still isn't anywhere near the point of marginal utility. One of the things that made it psychologically difficult to increase our giving was that for many years we were giving away a bigger slice of our income than anyone we knew. No one, not even the megarich, seemed to be giving a higher proportion.

Then in 2004 the *New Yorker* published a profile of Zell Kravinsky. Kravinsky had given almost his entire $45-million real estate fortune to charity. He did put some money into trust funds for his wife and children, but the children were attending public schools, and he and his family were living on about $60,000 a year. He still did not think he had done enough to help others, so he arranged with a nearby hospital to donate a kidney to a stranger. The article linked my then-thirty-two-year-old essay to Kravinsky's way of living and quoted him as saying, "It seems to me crystal clear that I should be giving all my money away and donating all of my time and energy."[2]

By this time I was teaching at Princeton, not far from where Kravinsky lived, so I invited him to speak to one of my classes, something he has done regularly ever since. Kravinsky is a brilliant man: he has one doctorate in education and another on the poetry of John Milton. He taught at the University of Pennsylvania before turning from academic life to real estate investment, so he is at home in the university environment. Despite his interest in poetry, he puts his altruism in mathematical terms. Quoting scientific studies that show the risk of dying as a result of making a kidney donation to be only 1 in 4,000, he says that not making the donation would have meant he valued his life at 4,000 times that of a stranger, a valuation he finds totally unjustified. He even told Ian Parker, the author of the *New Yorker* profile, that the reason many people don't understand his desire to donate a kidney is that "they don't understand math."

Around the time I was reading about Kravinsky I became aware of the work of Abhijit Banerjee and Esther Duflo, professors of economics at MIT, who founded the Poverty Action Lab to carry out "social experiments"—by which they meant empirical research to discover which interventions against poverty work and which do not. Without such evidence, Duflo points out, we are fighting poverty the way medieval doctors fought illness by applying leeches.[3] Banerjee and Duflo pioneered the application of randomized controlled trials, the golden standard of the pharmaceutical industry, to specific aid projects. By 2010 researchers associated with the Poverty Action Lab—now known as the Abdul Latif Jameel Poverty Action Lab, or J-PAL—had carried out 240 experiments in 40 countries. Dean Karlan, once a student of Banerjee and Duflo and now himself a professor of economics at Yale, started Innovations for Poverty Action, a nonprofit organization to bridge the gap between academic research and the practical side of development. Innovations for Poverty Action has grown to have a staff of nine hundred and a budget of $25 million, and the idea of randomized trials is clearly catching on.

In 2006 Holden Karnofsky and Elie Hassenfeld were in their midtwenties, working for a hedge fund in Connecticut, and earning far more than they had any desire to spend. Together with some of their colleagues, they talked about giving significant amounts to charity—but to which charity? (The Poverty Action Lab and Innovations for Poverty Action evaluate specific interventions, such as distributing bednets to protect people against malaria, but not the charitable organizations themselves, most of which have several programs.) Karnofsky, Hassenfeld, and their colleagues were used to analyzing large amounts of data in order to find sound investments. They contacted several charities and asked them what a donation would accomplish. They got lots of glossy brochures with pictures of smiling children but no data that told them what the charities were achieving and at what cost. Calling the charities and explaining what they wanted to know got them no further. One charity told them that the information they were seeking was confidential. Karnofsky and Hassenfeld sensed a vacuum that needed to be filled. With financial support from their colleagues, they set up GiveWell, an organization that has taken the evaluation of charities to a new level. They soon found they could not run it part-time and so left the hedge fund, a move that cut their income by more than half. Their assumption is that if enough people follow the recommendations on GiveWell's website, the charities will realize that it is in their interest to be transparent and to demonstrate their effectiveness. GiveWell estimates that in 2013 more than $17 million dollars went to its top-ranked charities as a result of those rankings. Although that is not enough to have a major impact on the charitable field as a whole, the figure has risen sharply each year since GiveWell was launched. GiveWell's existence has been critical to the development of the effective altruism movement. Now, when skeptics ask, How do I know that my donation will really help people in need? there is a good reply: If you give to one of GiveWell's top-rated charities, you can be confident that your donation will do good and be highly cost-effective.[4]

Around the time Karnofsky and Hassenfeld were setting up GiveWell, Toby Ord was studying philosophy at the University of Oxford. As an undergraduate, Ord, an Australian, had initially studied computer science and mathematics at the University of Melbourne, but he often got into arguments about ethical and political issues. When he expressed his views about poverty, his friends would retort, "If you believe that, why don't you just give most of your money to people starving in Africa?" His friends thought that this conclusion was absurd, but Toby asked himself, "If my money could help others much more than it helps me, then why not?"

Ord's growing interest in ethics led him to do a second undergraduate degree in philosophy. He did so well that he got a scholarship to Oxford, where he wrote a doctoral thesis on how we should decide what to do. He remained interested in practical ethics, and read my article "Famine, Affluence and Morality." He began to think seriously about what he could do for people in extreme poverty. At the time he was living quite comfortably on his graduate student scholarship, which paid him £14,000 a year, a sum that put him, he noticed, in the richest 4 percent of the world's people, even after adjusting for how much further money goes in developing countries.[5] When he graduated he would be earning more. He decided to calculate how much he would be able to give away over his lifetime, after meeting his own needs, assuming he earned a standard academic salary. His earnings, he estimated, might come to £1.5 million, or US$2.5 million (in 2005 dollars), and of this, he thought he could donate two-thirds, that is, £1 million, or US$1.7 million. Then he asked himself what that sum could achieve if it were donated to the most effective charities. He estimated that, while maintaining an attractive quality of life, he could donate enough to cure eighty thousand people of blindness or to save around fifty thousand years of healthy life.[6] In other words, his donations would achieve the equivalent of saving the lives of one thousand children, each of whom would live another fifty years in good health, or of enabling five thousand people to live an extra ten healthy years. Such benefits so dramatically outweighed the small sacrifice Ord imagined he would be making that he committed himself to living on £20,000 per annum (adjusted for inflation and equivalent to US$34,000) and giving away the rest. His wife, Bernadette Young, a physician, pledged to give away everything above £25,000 (US$42,600). Ord subsequently lowered his own allowance to £18,000 (US$30,600), as he found that £20,000 was more than he needed to live comfortably and even take a holiday in France or Italy.[7]

Ord wanted to share his knowledge of how easy it is to make a huge positive difference to the world. In 2009 he and Will MacAskill, another Oxford philosophy graduate student, founded Giving What We Can, an international society dedicated to eliminating poverty in the developing world. Members pledge to give at least 10 percent of their income to wherever they think it will do the most to relieve suffering in the developing world. At the time of writing, 644 people have taken the pledge, and Giving What We Can estimates that if the donors all do what they have pledged to do, $309 million will go to the most effective charities.[8]

In addition to helping Ord launch Giving What We Can, MacAskill had an idea for another organization. Students and other young people get plenty of career advice, but none of it is directed toward the question an effective altruist would ask: What career will enable me to do the most good over my lifetime? In 2011 MacAskill and five friends founded 80,000 Hours, so named because that is roughly the number of hours people spend working in their careers. 80,000 Hours does research on which careers do the most good, offers free career coaching, and is building a global community of people seeking to change the world for the better.[9] (Curious about the careers 80,000 Hours recommends? Wait for chapters 4 and 5.)

The term *effective altruism* was born when Giving What We Can and 80,000 Hours decided to apply for charitable status under a common umbrella organization. The umbrella organization needed a name. After tossing around some names, including High Impact Alliance and Evidence-based Charity Association, the group took a vote, and Centre for Effective Altruism was the clear winner. Effective altruism soon caught on and became the term for the entire movement.[10]

While these developments were taking place, I continued to write about our obligations to help people in great need. In 1999 and

2006 I published essays in the *New York Times Sunday Magazine*. The response to the second article was so positive that I developed it into a book, *The Life You Can Save*, which appeared in 2009. In the final chapter I suggested a progressive scale of giving, like a tax scale, where the amount you give increases as your income increases. As compared with Giving What You Can's flat 10 percent pledge, my suggestion is for a lower level of giving for average income earners but a higher one for those with high incomes. Agata Sagan, a Polish researcher and supporter of the ideas in the book, set up a website so that people can pledge online to meet the level of donation suggested for their income. So far, more than seventeen thousand people have taken this pledge. Gradually the website evolved into an organization, which really took off when I got an email from Charlie Bresler. Charlie and his wife, Diana Schott, are representative of those who, nearing the age when people traditionally retired from paid employment, are thinking about what they want to do with the next ten, twenty, or even thirty years of useful life they may still have left. As students in the sixties, Charlie and Diana had been active in the movement against the war in Vietnam and for a transformation of political life in the United States. When it became apparent that the system was more resistant to reform than they had hoped, Diana became a physician while Charlie earned a doctorate in psychology. After spending some time as a professor of psychology he stumbled—his word—into becoming president of Men's Wearhouse, a major national clothing chain. That increased his income, but in the back of their minds Charlie and Diana retained the idea that after they had raised their family they would do something to make the world a better place. Charlie read *The Life You Can Save* and decided that helping people in extreme poverty would be worthy of his time and energy. He is now the unpaid executive director of The Life You

Can Save. In 2013, the first year in which the organization was fully operational, it conservatively estimated that, on a budget of $147,000, it had moved $594,000 to highly effective charities, yielding a "return on investment" of more than 400 percent.[11]

PART TWO

HOW TO DO THE MOST GOOD

3

Living Modestly to Give More

Toby Ord's calculation of how much good he would be able to do over his lifetime shows that it is possible to do an immense amount of good without earning a lot. Julia Wise is an effective altruist who has managed, on quite a modest wage, to give surprisingly large amounts to effective charities. Her blog, Giving Gladly, provides insights into how she does it. She quotes a friend who said to her, "It sounds very dreary, living on rice and beans and never going out to a movie." She then explains that that isn't how she lives.[1]

Julia and her partner, Jeff Kaufman, met in college. They had little space or money, and much of their enjoyment came from spending time with their friends. When they married in 2009 they talked about how they would live and agreed that they would continue to live modestly so they could give something, even on a low income, and as their earnings increased they would give more. Julia is a social worker, and Jeff is a computer programmer. Their combined income was under $40,000 in 2008, but since then a sharp increase in Jeff's earnings has brought it to $261,416 for the year ending July 2014. In each of these years from 2008 to 2014, with one exception when Julia was saving to pay her way through graduate school, Julia and Jeff have donated at least a third of their income, and as their income rose they have given half. Julia made a diagram of what they did with their money in the year ending July 2014 (fig. 1).

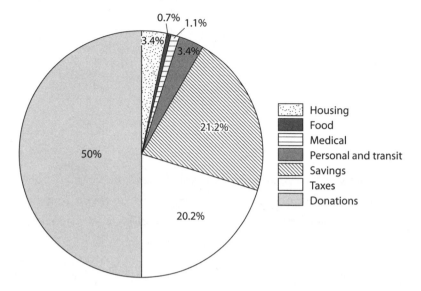

Fig. 1. Julia Wise and Jeff Kaufman's budget, August 2013–July 2014.

Julia and Jeff saved money by using public transit rather than owning a car. Their housing expenses are low because they rent part of a house, but they expect these costs to go up once they buy their own house. They are saving for that and also for retirement and future expenses related to their child. Nevertheless, they were able to donate half their income and plan to continue doing that in future.[2]

Julia realizes that she benefits because Jeff has above-average earnings, but she knows what it is like to live on not much more than the median income in the United States, as she and Jeff had to do it only a few years ago. So she offers a hypothetical model of what she might spend and donate if she were forced to live on the $35,000 she earned on her own in 2013–14, which is close to the median personal income in the United States (fig. 2).

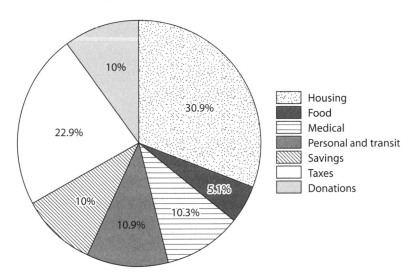

Fig. 2. Budget for a single person living in the Boston area
on $35,000 a year.

Julia offers the following as a realistic breakdown of expenses:

- $900 on rent and $100 on utilities each month (enough for a small apartment or an apartment shared with friends in the Boston area)
- $150 a month on groceries (more than Julia spends)
- $300 a month for health insurance and other medical costs
- $70 for a public transit pass
- $250 a month for personal spending (phone, clothes, entertainment, etc.)
- Saving 10 percent of income
- Donating 10 percent of income

A person living on the median income can, therefore, donate 10 percent to effective charities, save 10 percent for the future, and still have enough to live comfortably and enjoyably.

How Much Is Enough?

As a small child Julia Wise grasped that although she did not lack anything she needed, there were others who did. Ever since, she has seen every dollar she spends as a dollar taken out of the hands of someone who needs it more than she does. So the question she asks herself is not how much she should give, but how much she should keep.

Julia is not a Catholic, but her account of her early insight echoes the words of Ambrose, a fourth-century archbishop of Milan who was later canonized and became known as one of the four original Great Doctors of the Roman Catholic Church. Ambrose said that when you give to the poor, "You are not making a gift of your possessions to the poor person. You are handing over to him what is his. For what has been given in common for the use of all, you have arrogated to yourself."[3] That became part of the Christian tradition: Thomas Aquinas went so far as to say, "It is not theft, properly speaking, to take secretly and use another's property in a case of extreme need: because that which he takes for the support of his life becomes his own property by reason of that need."[4] Surprisingly to some, the Roman Catholic Church has never repudiated this radical view and has even reiterated it on several occasions. Pope Paul VI quoted the passage in which Ambrose says that what you give to the poor is really already theirs and added, in his encyclical *Populorum Progressio*, "We must repeat once more that the superfluous wealth of rich countries should be placed at the service of poor nations. The rule which up to now held good for the benefit of those nearest to us, must today be applied to all the needy of this world." On the twentieth anniversary of *Populorum Progressio*, Pope John Paul II said it again, in his encyclical *Sollicitudo Rei Socialis*, and Pope Francis has indicated his support for this doctrine too.[5] The problem is that these are just words until the Church puts the full weight of its moral authority behind them. Popes, bishops, and priests are quick to condemn supposed sins like the use of contraception, homosexual acts, and abortion, but they are much less willing to speak out against the blatant failures of wealthy Catholics to give to the poor what the Church says is owed to them.

The Church's teachings on poverty are in accord with the Gospel account of the reply Jesus gave to the rich man who told Jesus that he had, since childhood, kept all the commandments and wanted to know what else he should do to go to heaven. "One thing you lack," Jesus is described as having said to him. "Go, sell everything you have and give to the poor."[6] Aaron Moore, an Australian international aid worker and artist, is one of the relatively few Christians who have taken the words of Jesus seriously. On his website, Moore links them to a statement of mine: "If we can prevent something bad, without sacrificing anything of comparable significance, we ought to do it."[7] Aaron was not rich, by Australian standards—he didn't own a house or a car—but when he entered his income on www.globalrichlist.com, it told him he was in the top 1 percent of the world by income. So at the age of thirty-four, Aaron put all the larger items he owned—his motorbike, laptop, mobile phone, surfboard, wetsuit, and paintings—up for auction, with no reserve, and opening bids of one cent. They all sold. Most of the rest of his possessions were put on exhibit in a Sydney gallery space that was made to look like his home. Other items that he assumed would not sell, like his used underwear and his inscribed under–12 soccer trophies, were donated to the local Salvation Army store. Aaron gave the proceeds of the sale to the poor, along with all the money that was in his bank accounts. He left the gallery owning nothing but the clothes he was wearing. He wanted to experience what it would be like to put Jesus's words into action, and he hoped to start a discussion about the responsibilities of the affluent to the global poor. Is it okay, he asked, for us to be going to the movies and drinking chai lattes while 1.4 billion people are living in extreme poverty?[8]

Aaron's act was part symbolic statement and part experiment in living according to the words of Jesus. It was not intended to set a standard either for what everyone should do or for how he planned to live the rest of his life. Today, Aaron has a modest amount of possessions and sets aside a portion of his earnings to donate each month. That's more in keeping with effective altruism than with what Jesus said to the rich man, because giving *everything* one owns to the poor is going to make it hard to earn more and thus to give more. You need to dress respectably to get a job, and today you may need a laptop and a smartphone too. The best way of maximizing the amount you can give will depend on your individual circumstances and skills, but trying to live without at least a modest level of comfort and convenience is likely to be counterproductive.

Having Children

When Julia was young she felt so strongly that her choice to donate or not donate meant the difference between someone else living or dying that she decided it would be immoral for her to have children. They would take too much of her time and money. She told her father of her decision, and he replied. "It doesn't sound like this lifestyle is going to make you happy," to which she responded, "My happiness is not the point." Later, when she was with Jeff, she realized that her father was right. Her decision not to have a child was making her miserable. She talked to Jeff, and they decided they could afford to raise a child and still give plenty. The fact that Julia could look forward to being a parent renewed her sense of excitement about the future. She suspects that her satisfaction with her life makes her of more use to the world than she would be if she were "a broken-down altruist."

Everyone has boundaries. If you find yourself doing something that makes you bitter, it is time to reconsider. Is it possible for you to become more positive about it? If not, is it really for the best, all things considered? George Fox, the founder of the Society of Friends, also known as Quakers, urged his followers to be an example to others and to "walk cheerfully over the world." Julia refers to that thought, saying, "We don't need people making sacrifices that leave them drained and miserable. We need people who can walk cheerfully over the world, or at least do their damnedest."[9] There are still relatively few effective altruists, so it is important that they set an example that attracts others to this way of living. Julia spoke to my class at Princeton, and she did present a cheerful image of a person thoroughly enjoying her chosen lifestyle.[10] She referred to the ability she and Jeff have to save hundreds of lives and improve many more as "an amazing opportunity."[11] In responding to a question asked by a student, she said she does not tell others who spend a lot on themselves and give nothing away that their lifestyle is immoral because, "you can't change people by preaching at them."

Julia admits to making mistakes. When shopping, she would constantly ask herself, "Do I need this ice cream as much as a woman living in poverty elsewhere in the world needs to get her child vaccinated?" That made grocery shopping a maddening experience, so she and Jeff made a decision about what they would give away over the next six months and then drew up a budget based on what was left. Within that budget, they regarded the money as theirs, to spend on themselves. Now Julia doesn't scrimp on ice cream because, as she told the class, "Ice cream is really important to my happiness."

Another error was telling her parents and her grandmother that she did not want Christmas presents and would sell them if they gave her any. That made her grandmother, in particular, really unhappy. Julia is not so hard-line now. At first her financially conservative parents had some concerns about how much she and Jeff were giving away, but once they saw that Julia was not, as they had feared, "living in a cardboard box" they became more positive about it.

For both Jeff and herself, Julia says, strong social ties to family and to friends are a basic source of happiness. (No surprise there, as most studies of happiness reach the same conclusion.) Julia and Jeff have other sources of enjoyment that cost little or nothing: "Cooking, walking, playing board games, and making music with family and friends." Julia and Jeff began leading an effective altruism discussion group, and the development of a community of effective altruists in the Boston area has given them a new source of pleasure: meeting people who think as they do and continuing to have the kind of deep, stimulating conversations many people have only during their university days.[12]

Julia's and Jeff's decision to have a child shows that they drew a line beyond which they would not let the goal of maximizing their giving prevent them from having something very important to them. Bernadette Young, Toby Ord's partner, has described their decision to have a child in a similar way: "I'm happy donating 50 percent of my income over my life, but if I also chose not to have a child simply to raise that amount to 55 percent, then that final 5 percent would cost me more than all the rest. . . . I'm deciding to meet a major psychological need and to plan a life I can continue to live in the long term." Neither Julia nor Bernadette is unusual in experiencing the inability to have a child—for whatever reason—as deeply distressing.[13] Having a child undoubtedly takes both money and time, but against this, Bernadette points out, effective altruists can reasonably hope that having a child will benefit the world. Both cognitive abilities and characteristics like empathy have a significant inherited component, and we can also expect that children will be influenced by the values their parents hold and practice in their daily lives. Although there can be no certainty that the children of effective altruists will, over their lifetimes, do more good than harm, there is a reasonable probability that they will, and this helps to offset the extra costs of raising them.[14] We can put it another way: If all those who are concerned to do the most good decide not to have children, while those who do not care about anyone else continue to have children, can we really expect that, a few generations on, the world will be a better place than it would have been if those who care about others had had children?

As the time for the birth of Julia's daughter neared, she speculated on how being a mother would change her. Some of her friends had suggested that once she had her own child she would not keep up her level of giving. Julia replied that her daughter will not want for anything she really needs, but she rejected the idea that her responsibility is limited to doing her best for her own child. Having her own child, she said, would bring her closer to "the Other Woman"—the mother who has to struggle to give her child clean water and enough to eat. That woman, she knew, loves her child as she loves her own.[15]

Meet Some More Effective Altruists

In the remainder of this chapter and the one that follows I introduce you to several more effective altruists. My aim is to show that, notwithstanding the skepticism about altruism mentioned in the preface, many diverse kinds of people become effective altruists. In addition, these brief sketches will provide a basis for my subsequent exploration, in chapters 6, 7, and 8, of what motivates effective altruists and how they feel about the change that effective altruism has brought to their lives.

Rhema Hokama demonstrates what it is like to be an effective altruist on a very modest income. She heard of effective altruism during her later years in college and decided she would start giving when she got her first paycheck. She is studying for her doctorate in English literature at Harvard, and her income from teaching, research stipends, and freelance editorial and writing work amounts to around $27,000 a year.

Rhema began by donating 2 percent of her income and has gradually been increasing that percentage. At the time of writing, it is 5 percent. She has set up a separate donation account, and each month, on receiving her salary, she transfers 5 percent to that account. At the end of the year, she will donate it.

Rents are high in Cambridge, Massachusetts, where Harvard University is located, so to live within her salary and still have something to give, Rhema rents an apartment outside the city but close enough to where she works that she doesn't need to own a car. Instead, she walks, rides a bike, or uses public transport. Unlike many of her colleagues, she brings her lunch from home rather than eating out.

Rhema thinks her income, even after giving, is quite adequate. She likes to remind herself that it is sixteen times the average global income of $1,680 a year and places her in the world's richest 4.4 percent.[16] In other words, of the world's approximately 7.2 billion people, about 6.9 billion of them earn less than Rhema does. In any case, the income Rhema now earns is comparable to her household income when she was growing up in Hawaii, where she was born into a large working family—the children and grandchildren of pineapple and sugarcane plantation workers. Her relatives now work as hotel busboys, office assistants, newspaper distributors, construction workers, warehouse truck drivers, privates in the U.S. Army, call operators, grocery cashiers, nurses, and servers at McDonald's. Growing up, she didn't know anyone who made more than $50,000 a year. At Harvard she knows very few people who grew up in a family making less than $100,000 a year, and her friends and colleagues can't really imagine living on less than they have. One of them, earning an amount similar to Rhema's, complained that she was living below the poverty line when in fact she was earning almost three times the United States poverty line of $11,490 for a single person.

Rhema has donated to Oxfam and the International Planned Parenthood Federation. Last year she donated to the Fistula Foundation, which, for about $450, performs surgery to repair obstetric fistulas—a condition that causes young women who have had problems during labor to leak urine and feces through the vagina, as a result of which they often become social outcasts for the rest of their lives. Rhema says that "giving back a portion of my earnings is the least I can do to help other women receive the necessary surgeries for injuries that are almost nonexistent in the developed world." She acknowledges feeling that her good fortune "is not fundamentally the product of my own doing." Giving helps relieve any guilt that might arise from that thought because it makes Rhema feel that "in some small way, I'm working toward building the kind of world I would want to live in."[17]

When Celso Vieira was a child growing up in a small city in Brazil, his parents were told he had a cognitive disability, probably autism. The signs were clear: he speaks slowly, uses language in an odd way, and cannot look people in the eye. His parents were advised to put him in a special school. Instead, they bribed the director of a local normal school to accept him. To everyone's surprise, his grades always put him at the top of his class. He now speaks nine languages and is writing a thesis on Plato for his doctorate in philosophy. In 2008, after reading my *Practical Ethics*, he became a vegan and started donating 10 percent of his modest income, at first to Unicef and Oxfam, but later, after doing more research on effectiveness, to other charities, including Innovations for Poverty Action. He plans to raise his level of donations to 20 percent. He lives very simply, not only to have more to donate but also to reduce his impact on the environment. He rents a room in a shared house and has no television or refrigerator. He eats grains and fresh vegetables. In 2014, when he moved to a different place to live, his possessions consisted of a mattress, a guitar, a skateboard, a computer, a chair, a tiny table, and a backpack that contained all his clothes except the ones he was wearing.

In addition to writing his thesis, studying a language, practicing his guitar, and writing children's books, a novel for adults, short stories, and a translation of Plato's *Cratylus* that preserves the puns most translators consider to be untranslatable, Celso is an effective altruist. In Belo Horizonte, where he lives, he started the first Brazilian chapter of The Life You Can Save. The group encourages people to pledge to donate to effective charities, holds fund-raising events, and devises strategies to make it easier for them to fulfill their pledges.

Celso is an example of the spread of effective altruism beyond its origins in the United Kingdom and the United States. His unusual personality also affords insights that improve our understanding of the motives of effective altruists, which I shall examine in chapters 7 and 8. Celso is, as he says, "more moved by arguments than by empathy." He has come to effective altruism through reasoning about what he ought to do.

Priya Basil followed a more fortuitous path to effective altruism. She knows both poor countries and rich ones, for she grew up in Kenya, though in what she describes as "a bubble of privilege." Her grandparents did not have it so easy. They came from India during the period of the British Raj to work on building the Kenyan rail-ways. Her parents were born in Kenya but moved to the United Kingdom after Kenya became independent. They were educated in Britain and returned to Kenya when Priya was a baby. Despite being surrounded by extreme poverty, Priya did not reflect on the inequal-ity she saw. It was only when she was in her late teens that a sudden collapse in her family's fortunes made her face up to the unfair dis-tribution of wealth. Her family returned to Britain, where she went to university and studied literature and then got a job in advertising. Though now more aware of the suffering of others, she still didn't think it was incumbent on her to alleviate it. That changed when she fell in love with a man who believes we all have a responsibility to make the world better. She moved to Germany to live with him and started to write her first novel, *Ishq and Mushq*. Now she was com-pelled to live frugally, and that gave her a sense of how it was possible to be happy—perhaps even happier—with less. Her writing drew on her immigrant background, which led her to confront the ignorance of her childhood and adolescence in Kenya. In this frame of mind she read *The Life You Can Save* and took the pledge on the website. Her second novel, *The Obscure Logic of the Heart*, refers to some of the ideas that led her to give, and she is currently writing a third novel that will also express ideas related to effective altruism.

Perhaps because of her own path to effective altruism, Priya is acutely aware of the fact that the circumstances we're in and the people around us play a big role in determining our values and behavior. She admits that, as she puts it, "my default setting is 'Me First' and it's a constant struggle not to let this impulse override every decision." Given that and her susceptibility to the temptations of shopping, she feels it is easier for her to be a better person more of the time in Germany than in the United Kingdom because consumption in Germany is not quite as brazen as in Britain (she hasn't lived in the United States!). At the same time, she believes, "altruism needs to be watched, challenged and nurtured, otherwise it risks becoming stale and automatic." She has been giving 5 percent of her income to effective charities, with something of a bias toward charities working in Kenya because of her connections there. That level of giving, for someone on her income, meets the requirements of The Life You Can Save pledge, but Priya is pushing herself to increase it to 10 percent. In addition to giving, Priya and her partner cofounded an organization called Authors for Peace, and she has been involved in other political initiatives, including Writers Against Mass Surveillance. Although she acknowledges that the effectiveness of these political initiatives is difficult to determine, she believes that by working to better any one society we increase the chance of betterment for all societies.

Effective altruism is something for people of many divergent backgrounds and for people who, while living in affluent societies, earn no more and sometimes even less than the average income in their society. They can, by giving, say, 10 percent of their income to effective charities, save lives or restore sight or in other ways make a huge difference to the lives of people who may be living on an income that is, in purchasing power, the equivalent of as little as 1 or 2 percent of the median income in the United States.

4

Earning to Give

Although it is possible to earn an average income and still donate enough to do a lot of good, it remains true that the more you earn, the more you can donate. That idea, which led Matt Wage to his current career, must have occurred to many people before the effective altruism movement existed. In the eighteenth century John Wesley, the founder of Methodism, told his congregations to "earn all you can, give all you can, save all you can."[1] Another was Jim Greenbaum, who heard the term *effective altruism* when viewing, on TED.com, a talk I had given in 2013. He realized that now there is a name for what he had been doing for most of his life. Because Jim has been quite deliberately earning money in order to be able to give money away for longer than anyone else I know, his life demonstrates that this can be done successfully over several decades.

Jim was born in 1958 and grew up in a Jewish family living in Louisiana, in the heart of America's Bible Belt. As a child, he recalls, "when something didn't seem reasonable, logical, or fair, I'd fight against it." He saw footage of the Nazi concentration camps and heard rabbis give sermons and say, "Never again!" They would condemn the Allies for doing nothing to stop the Holocaust, while newspapers carried stories of atrocities still being committed around the world. The hypocrisy began to gnaw at him, and that influence can still be seen in a line he uses on the website of the foundation he set up: "Being a bystander to suffering is not an option."

When Jim graduated from college, he was thinking of going to law school with the goal of practicing civil rights law. But he didn't get into the top law schools and didn't fancy another three years' study somewhere that was not at the highest level, so he decided to go into business, make money quickly, and use it to change the world. After some false starts, he founded Access Long Distance, which grew into a nationwide telecommunications company. In 1990, when Jim was thirty-two, he happened to catch a television program about an American who had gone to Romania to help orphans who were living in atrocious conditions. Jim set himself a deadline: eight more years in business would take him to forty, and then he would quit and start using his money to help others. He missed the deadline but not by much: when he sold his company in 1999 he had just turned forty-one, and his net worth was about to peak at $133 million. He has committed to contributing 85 percent of that during his lifetime to projects aimed at reducing the suffering of both humans and nonhuman animals, with the remainder of his wealth going to the same purpose after his death. So far he has contributed more than $40 million to the Greenbaum Foundation, which he runs together with his wife, Lucie Berreby-Greenbaum. The foundation has supported projects aimed at preventing and alleviating animal suffering and abuse, improving health in developing countries, educating people in Africa about human rights, and rescuing victims of human trafficking for sex and labor.

Compared to the other effective altruists we have met, Jim lives an affluent life and lives in a luxurious home. He once owned a few sports cars and a share in a private jet but soon came to see those as excesses. While he now drives a Toyota, he still struggles to find a balance between his lifestyle and using his money to help others. As early as 2003, before effectiveness was as widely talked about as it is today, Jim was mostly supporting overseas projects. When he was asked for donations to local projects, he would say, "I can give you this much money, or I can save this many lives. You tell me what to do."[2] Nevertheless, he is very conscious of the need, when motivating wealthy people to give, to start where they are, so he accepts some "ineffective passion" in their giving, as long as at least half goes to effective giving.

How does earning a lot of money and giving a lot away compare with becoming an aid worker for an effective charity? Will MacAskill puts forward this argument: Suppose you could have worked for an effective charity but instead you accept a job with an investment bank that pays you $200,000 a year. There is usually no shortage of applicants for jobs with charities, so the charity will appoint someone else who will probably do almost as good a job as you would have done. "Almost" because if you had been offered the job, we can assume the charity considered you the best applicant for the position; but the difference between you and the next-best applicant is unlikely to be great. As a charity worker, therefore, you are largely replaceable. Working in finance, however, you earn much more than you need and give half of your earnings to the charity, which can use that money to employ two extra workers it would not, without your donation, have been able to employ at all. The amount of work they can do for the charity will greatly exceed the difference between what you would have done and what the next-best applicant for your position will do. Whereas you would have been replaceable as a charity worker, you are not replaceable as a donor. If you had not taken the job with the investment bank, someone else would have and almost certainly would not have donated half of her or his salary to charity (very few people in the finance sector do). So if you take the finance job, the charity will be better able to achieve its aims than it would have been if you had accepted their offer of employment.[3]

Will also points out that we sometimes learn that a charity is not as effective as we thought it was. Donors can then easily switch their giving to a better charity. If you are already working for the charity when you find out that it is not particularly effective, however, it will not be easy to find a new job with the most effective charity. If you are able to change the charity that employs you, making it more effective than it was, you may have a bigger impact still; but many organizations, whether charities or not, are resistant to change.

Notwithstanding exceptions like Jim Greenbaum, most of those earning to give are from the generation that started to think about their career choices around the turn of the millennium. They have been prepared to go in new directions. In the nineties if you had said that you were going into finance in order to earn more to give more, people would have looked at you oddly, and you would have felt very alone in what you were doing. For millennials, however, connecting with like-minded people via social media comes naturally. So it is easy to find websites on which you can exchange experiences with people like Aveek Bhattacharya, who put aside plans for an academic career in order to earn more and donate more with a London-based firm of strategy consultants. Or you may meet Alex Foster, whose Christian beliefs led him to want to do something about poverty. Alex is now launching his own company and is committed to donating everything he earns above £15,000 a year.[4] If you are earning to give in order to reduce animal suffering, you can discuss the best options with Simon Knutson, who works for an investment company in Gothenburg, Sweden, and donates about 40 percent of his after-tax income to support Animal Charity Evaluators, which tries to find the most effective charities helping animals. Ben West, after being employed as a software developer in Madison, Wisconsin, started his own company in order to be able to donate more. He gives to Animal Charity Evaluators and the Global Priorities Project at the University of Oxford's Future of Humanity Institute, which investigates the problem of how to allocate scarce resources among different global needs.

In the popular mind, altruism would not rank high among the characteristics of a professional poker player. That may be about to change. Philipp Gruissem won enough at poker to live the kind of life that celebrity magazines encourage us to fantasize about. For five years he was able to travel where he wanted and enjoyed the freedom to experience life in many ways. The time came, though, when he realized that the life he was leading was not satisfying him. To be happy, he needed some larger purpose in his life. Swiss friends introduced him to effective altruism, and he found a new motivation for playing poker that led him to his biggest wins, including a total of nearly $2.4 million in two tournaments in 2013. Now Gruissem is spreading effective charity among other professional poker players with a new organization called Raising for Effective Giving.[5]

These people are all giving far beyond conventional standards of philanthropy, but of all the effective altruists I have encountered, Ian Ross offers the most remarkable example of a life committed to maximizing giving. Ian started working full-time in 2006 and between then and the time of writing has donated or earmarked for future donation about $1 million. In 2014 he earned more than $400,000, and more than 95 percent of his after-tax earnings goes to charities. The ethical motivation for Ian's lifestyle began in college, when he became a vegan. For the best part of the next decade, a friend, also vegan, subjected him to merciless cross-examination. The outcome was that Ian came to accept the following argument:

1. Modern animal agriculture causes an immense amount of suffering.
2. We are responsible both for what we do and for what we refrain from doing.
3. We have the means to reduce the suffering caused by modern animal agriculture. Therefore:
4. It is imperative for each of us to do so.

Ian then began to put that logic into practice in his own life. He worked for four years at McKinsey, the management consultants, and then at the Disney Corporation before moving to a more senior role in a video gaming startup. Outside his day job, Ian helped start Hampton Creek Foods, which produces plant-based egg substitutes that are already cutting into the demand for eggs from caged hens. The majority of his donations go to organizations like the Humane League and Mercy for Animals because their education and outreach campaigns have been shown to be effective in encouraging people to stop eating animal products. Ian also gives to global public health organizations like Population Services International because he sees bringing family planning to people without access to it as win-win, preventing the birth of unwanted children and giving adults more control over their lives. At the same time, because most humans eat meat, fewer children means less demand for animal products, which in turn reduces animal suffering.

Ian can focus on his goal of reducing suffering because he doesn't have a partner or children and has no plans to change that situation. He doesn't see this as a sacrifice because his lack of interest in having a partner predates his effort to follow his ethical ideas to their logical conclusions. He plays soccer with friends, enjoys listening to music, and goes cycling most weekends, all within an annual budget of around $9,000. Outside that budget, though, he did spend $8,000 to pay the veterinary expenses for the companion animal of a friend with whom he is very close. He admits he can't really justify this, so he considers it a kind of "luxury spending."

The Psychology of Earning to Give

In 2013 an article in the *Washington Post* featured Jason Trigg, an MIT computer science graduate working in finance and giving half of his salary to the Against Malaria Foundation. Trigg was described as part of "an emerging class of young professionals in America and Britain" for whom "making gobs of money is the surest way to save the world."[6] In the *New York Times* the columnist David Brooks wrote that Trigg seemed to be "an earnest, morally serious young man" who might well save many lives. Nevertheless, Brooks urged caution. He warned, first, that our daily activities change us, and by working in a hedge fund your ideals could slip so that you become less committed to giving. Second, he thought that choosing a profession that does not arouse your passion for the sake of an "abstract, faraway good" might leave you loving humanity in general but not the particular humans around you. Third, and most important, Brooks worried about "turning yourself into a means rather than an end . . . a machine for the redistribution of wealth." Taking a job just to make money could be "corrosive," Brooks wrote, even if you use the money for charity.[7]

The first two objections make factual psychological claims that can be checked against people who are earning to give. The third objection is moral, rather than psychological, so I will postpone discussion of it until we come to ethical objections in the next section.

In 2013 Matt Wage spoke to the Princeton class he had taken four years earlier. He told the students that when he went to work in finance some people raised concerns about his unusual choice. One worry was that an idealistic young person surrounded by cutthroat bankers wouldn't be able to handle the pressure and would quit. That hadn't happened. Matt doesn't regard the people he works with as cutthroats, and he finds the work itself interesting. The other major concern was one that Brooks mentions, which Matt put as follows: "By being around a lot of wealthy people who drive Ferraris, I would soon say, never mind about the charities, what I *really* want is a Ferrari." A Ferrari is still not on Matt's shopping list. His strategy for trying to prevent it ever getting there is to be very public about his pledge to donate 50 percent of his income. He has told all his friends that if he doesn't keep his pledge, they should ridicule him. (He has also given permission for his pledge to be mentioned in this book, making it even more public.) Overall, though, Matt gave no signs of being under any unusual psychological burden caused by earning to give. "I'm extremely happy with my life," he told me. "I'd still do this altruistic stuff even if I thought it was making my life worse, but, by a strange coincidence about how human minds work, I think it's actually making me happier."

Jim Greenbaum found his initial years frustrating, but only because it was taking him longer than he expected to create the wealth he needed to help others. It did not make him less committed to his ultimate goal. He enjoyed business, which in some ways seemed to him like a game. He also valued the people with whom he worked. He advocates balance between a comfortable life and doing good. Jim has already given away so much that his decision to earn money in order to give it away has obviously worked out very well.

Ben West points out that even from a selfish perspective, earning to give allows you to have things that people believe make them happy, like money and a high-status job, while still getting the fulfillment that comes from knowing you are helping to make the world a better place. Ian Ross doesn't see any risk of burnout and anticipates continuing along his current path. Alex Foster may be the most enthusiastic of all the earning-to-give people I have had contact with: he says he finds his career "insanely fulfilling—more satisfaction than any other period of my life. Despite heavily reduced social life." On the other hand, Aveek Bhattacharya is sometimes frustrated that his work does not allow him to probe issues as deeply as he would like. He always saw earning to give as an experiment, and, to him, the possibility of doing a doctorate and having an academic career remains open.[8]

Brooks would be on solid ground if he were merely warning his readers that earning to give is not for everyone. Some people can't work up much enthusiasm for making profits for their employer. Others, however, seem to enjoy earning money and thrive on the extra motivation provided by giving a large slice of it to good causes. They thus avoid the problem nicely summed up in a *New Yorker* cartoon in which a businessman on the phone complains, "I'm working harder than I ever have, but all I get out of it is larger and larger paychecks."[9]

Brooks speculates on the damage that could flow from turning yourself into a means for the redistribution of wealth, overlooking the fact that it is, unfortunately, the fate of many people to spend their lives supporting themselves and their families by doing work they do not find intrinsically interesting or enjoyable. Why would such work have a more corrosive effect on you if you are doing it in order to help others rather than to help yourself and your family?

The Ethics of Earning to Give

When Brooks objects to earning to give on the grounds that you are turning yourself into a means rather than an end, he is echoing an objection to utilitarianism made forty years earlier by the British philosopher Bernard Williams. Williams, in a critique of utilitarianism, asks us to imagine that George, an unemployed man with a chemistry degree, is offered a position in a laboratory developing new forms of chemical weapons. (Williams was writing before chemical weapons were banned by international treaty.) George is opposed to the development of chemical weapons, but if he does not take the job it will go to someone who will be much more zealous in pursuing the research than he would have been, and the outcome of George's rejection of the offer is likely to mean more, not fewer, new forms of chemical weapons.[10] If George is to do the most good, he must take the job, keeping his views about chemical weapons to himself while doing as little as possible to advance the goal for which he is being paid to work. To retain his position, however, he will have to do some things that advance the development of new chemical weapons. He may feel bad about that, but a utilitarian can reassure him that what really matters is that fewer deadly weapons will be developed.

Williams objects that George is being forced to "step aside from his own project and decision and acknowledge the decision which utilitarian calculation requires." To do such a thing, Williams argues, would alienate him from his actions and his convictions, with which he identifies, and is, "in the most literal sense, an attack on his integrity."[11] Is this true? And if it is, is there a parallel with what those who earn to give are doing when they choose to go into a profession they do not regard as intrinsically desirable? Investment banking is not morally on a par with developing chemical weapons. Nor would people who earn to give be deliberately working against the aims of their employer, as George would have been. On the contrary, they would want to do as well as possible so as to receive the highest possible salary and bonus and be able to donate the most. Nevertheless, to fit into the ethos of the organization in which they want to succeed, people earning to give may have to disguise their views about the intrinsic value of their work. It is also true that some of those who change their career in order to earn to give have stepped aside from their own projects (as Matt stepped aside from his original plan of going to graduate school and becoming a professor) and have instead taken the career required by "utilitarian calculation." But does this really mean, as Williams asserts, that they are alienated from their convictions and have lost their integrity? Does it, as Brooks suggests, turn you into a mere means to an end, with corrosive effects on your character?

Those who earn to give are, to a greater extent than most people, living in accord with their values—that is, with their core conviction that we ought to live our lives so as to do the most good we can. It is hard to see any alienation or loss of integrity here. On the contrary, for people who share that conviction, integrity would be lost if they were to follow their passion to, let's say, go to graduate school, write a thesis on *Beowulf*, and become a professor of medieval literature.[12]

Perhaps people who earn to give have integrity, yet they may be participating in activities that do harm? One critic puts it like this: "Capitalism in its current global form is worsening inequality. . . . A few people are gaining more wealth while many, many more are driven to more extreme poverty as a symptom of the market. The gap is widening between the very rich and very poor. . . . [W]orking in the financial industry in order to give to global poverty charities is akin to arsonists giving donations to the local fire department."[13]

Capitalism does appear to be increasing inequality, but that does not prove that it is driving people into extreme poverty because inequality can also increase when the rich become richer and the poor stay the same, or even when the poor gain but not by as much as the rich. As we saw in the preface, effective altruists typically value equality not for its own sake but only because of its consequences.[14] It isn't clear that making the rich richer without making the poor poorer has bad consequences, overall. It increases the ability of the rich to help the poor, and some of the world's richest people, including Bill Gates and Warren Buffett, have done precisely that, becoming, in terms of the amount of money given, the greatest effective altruists in human history. No doubt capitalism does drive some people into extreme poverty—it is such a vast system that it would be surprising if it did not—but it has also lifted hundreds of millions out of extreme poverty. It would not be easy to demonstrate that capitalism has driven more people into extreme poverty than it has lifted out of it; indeed there are good grounds for thinking that the opposite is the case.[15]

In any case, those who think the entire modern capitalist economy should be overthrown have conspicuously failed to demonstrate that there are ways of structuring an economy that have better outcomes. Neither have they indicated how, in the twenty-first century, a transition to an alternative economic system might occur. Like it or not, for the foreseeable future we seem to be stuck with some variety of capitalism, and along with it come markets in stocks, bonds, and commodities. These markets serve a variety of roles, including raising investment capital, reducing risk, and smoothing out swings in commodity prices. They don't seem inherently evil.

Granting that earning to give may lead to being involved in financial activities that harm some people does not settle the moral question of what the individual who has the opportunity to earn a lot and give a lot should do. Moral codes of behavior often give the principle "Do no harm" priority over the principle "Do the most good you can." Those who take this view will consider it wrong to work for a corporation that is harming innocent people, even if the good that one can then do would hugely outweigh this harm. The moral issue that lies behind this attitude arose in a dramatic form during World War II, when the Nazis were aiming their V–1 and V–2 rockets at London. Spies in London were sending them information about the accuracy of the attacks, but the spies were in fact British double agents, and the information was designed to mislead the Germans so that fewer rockets would hit London. It was estimated that this would save 12,000 casualties a month. When the British War Cabinet learned of the deception, in August 1944, Herbert Morrison, a minister and member of the Cabinet, objected that it was morally wrong for the government to determine that people living south of London would be killed rather than people living in central London. The do-no-harm principle seems to underlie this objection, for otherwise the good of preventing many deaths, by causing rockets to fall in rural areas, where they would do less damage, would have outweighed the harm of causing some deaths. Morrison was able to persuade the Cabinet to agree with him (Churchill was abroad at the time), but MI5, the British Security Service, managed to ignore Cabinet's decision and continue the deception until the end of the war.[16] If you think Morrison was right, you will probably also think that it is wrong to be involved in financial activities that harm some people, even if that brings about an equivalent benefit to many more. An effective altruist could take this view and still do a great deal of good while complying with the constraint of not doing harm. My own view, however, is that Morrison was wrong, and it was right to save the lives of many civilians.

The other relevant issue here is what we are to regard as being wrongfully complicit in a harm. For someone who judges actions by their consequences, to be complicit in wrongful harm requires that one make a difference to the likelihood of the harm occurring. As we saw earlier, if you do not take the position offered by the investment bank, someone else will, and from the bank's perspective that person will probably be nearly as good as you would have been. If one of the bank's capital-raising activities is funding a mine that is polluting a river on which many impoverished villagers depend, your refusal to take the job is not going to stop that happening. It will prevent you being able to donate as much to good causes, however, including charities that empower the weak so that they can better resist the depredations of mining companies. Moreover, you may have a better chance of altering the bank's actions—or, through the bank, the actions of the corporation for which it is raising money—if you are on the inside than if you are protesting from outside. You may find, on the other hand, that you cannot have any influence on the bank's policies because the corporate culture is to pursue profit regardless of the cost to the poor, and one junior employee cannot counteract that. Perhaps in especially egregious cases the right choice will be to quit and blow the whistle on what the bank is doing. Even then, your choice to work for the bank will have had good consequences, for it will have made you a better-informed, more credible opponent of the bank's actions.

The consequentialist notion of complicity does have implications that many people will reject. It implies, for instance, that the guards at Auschwitz were not acting wrongly if their refusal to serve in that role would have led only to their replacement by someone else, perhaps someone who would have been even more brutal toward those who were about to be murdered there. Given that serving as a concentration camp guard was often an alternative to being sent to the Russian front, this hypothetical was probably sometimes true. One might argue that, rather than accept this implication, we should consider not the actual consequences of one person's refusal to be a concentration camp guard but the consequences of everyone following a rule against acting for an institution engaged in wrongdoing. A Kantian might take that view, as would a rule-utilitarian—that is, someone who thinks it wrong to violate a rule if general acceptance of the rule would have good consequences.[17] We might also accept a different view of wrongful complicity, one that makes me responsible for the harm done by a group, organization, or other collective in which I intentionally participate.[18] Strictly utilitarian effective altruists could not accept these views and so would have to accept the implication that, on a plausible reading of the relevant facts, at least some of the guards at Auschwitz were not acting wrongly. It is possible to combine general support for effective altruism with acceptance of rule-utilitarianism or with another notion of complicity that is not consequentialist at all. If one did so and also held that investment banks and similar corporations are engaged in wrongdoing, one might see this as a sufficient reason for not going into the finance industry.[19] One might also take the view that the normal functions of an investment bank serve a beneficial economic purpose, and there is no need to assume that by going into banking one will be complicit in wrongdoing at all.

I suspect that in a decade or two, as we get more experience with earning to give, the ethical objections Brooks and others make to the practice will come to be seen as typical of the grumblings of an older generation that does not really understand what the next generation is doing. A Brookings Institution study has pointed out that millennials are much more concerned about corporate social responsibility than any previous generation, and as employees, they want "their daily work to be part of, and reflect, their societal concerns."[20] There are many ways of achieving that integration between work and social values. For the right person in the right circumstances, earning to give is one of them.

5

Other Ethical Careers

Earning to give is a distinctive way of doing good. For those with the abilities required for successfully earning to give, including the ability to find the work sufficiently interesting to do it well and the character to maintain a strong commitment to giving much of what one earns to effective charities, earning to give can be an ethical career choice. Nevertheless, Will MacAskill does not claim that earning to give is always or even usually the best option. Rather, he thinks we should see it as a baseline against which to compare other possible ethical careers.[1]

The Advocate

Will isn't in finance. That's because he believes that if he can influence two other people with earning capacities similar to his own to earn to give, he will have done more good than if he had gone into finance himself—and he has already influenced many more than two. 80,000 Hours is a metacharity, a charity that evaluates or promotes other charities. Other metacharities include Giving What We Can, GiveWell, and The Life You Can Save. Working for an effective metacharity can do more good than working for an ordinary charity because of the multiplier effect it can have—although this could also be an argument for earning to give and donating to the metacharity.

As in the case of an ordinary charity, you could be replaceable, but if you have special skills that others do not have, the payoff from those skills is likely to be high. Will's understanding of ethics, his argumentative skills, his experience with the effective altruism movement, his knowledge of the facts that underpin effective altruism, and his personal connections in the movement make him extremely difficult to replace.

The Bureaucrat

In the 1990s someone I will call Gorby (not his real name, as he wishes to remain anonymous) read "Famine, Affluence and Morality" and wrote to me for advice on his career choice. He had just finished graduate school, was volunteering for a charity, and living very cheaply, but he had realized that he might be able to do more good if instead of donating his time to the charity he worked for a bank and donated most of his earnings to it. Gorby also mentioned the possibility of working for the World Bank but dismissed that option because of the damage he believed the bank was doing to the very people he wanted to help. In the margins of his letter (this was pre-email) I scribbled a reply suggesting the possibility of being "a Gorbachev at the World Bank" and helping to reform it. I mailed his letter with my comments back to him and forgot all about it.

Years later I heard from Gorby again. He had joined the World Bank and was working with a team that evaluated the cost-effectiveness of the bank's investments in global health. More specifically, he was managing the section that recommended investments in family planning. As a result of the recommendations his section made, the bank shifted about $400 million from projects that cost $300 for each unwanted birth averted to projects that cost $50 for the same outcome. As this example shows, there are very big differences in the cost-effectiveness of different ways of improving the health of people in developing countries, so even with a fixed budget, better choices can make a huge difference. What Gorby's section did was equivalent, in the number of unwanted births averted, to adding $2 billion to the bank's family planning budget.

Gorby encourages others to follow his path because at organizations like the World Bank one has a very good chance of being in a position to control more money than one could realistically hope to earn by becoming wealthy. Moreover, he says, there is less competition for positions in such institutions than there is for high-earning jobs in the private sector, so one does not have to be exceptionally talented or work seventy-hour weeks in order to reach a level at which one can make a real difference. I don't really know if that is true, as Gorby is very bright indeed. But it is true that a career as a government bureaucrat or in a large international institution is not likely to be as glamorous or as well paid as a career in finance, so that may make it easier to rise through the ranks.

Researchers

For those with particular abilities in research, there may be special opportunities to do a great amount of good by a career in research. Most probably, though, this will not be in the obvious fields, like finding a vaccine for malaria or breeding better varieties of food crops. In the past, medical researchers have made discoveries that dramatically reduced or eliminated diseases like polio and smallpox, while the biologist Norman Borlaug, who bred the high-yielding grain varieties that led to the Green Revolution, is said to have saved more lives than anyone who has ever lived.[2] The impressive and highly publicized successes of scientists in these fields have drawn many highly talented researchers into the same areas of research, so the chances are small that any individual—such as you—will be able to make important discoveries that would not otherwise have been made. There may be better prospects of making an impact in a relatively uncrowded field. That is why 80,000 Hours recommends "Prioritization Research," which it describes as "activity aimed at working out which causes, interventions, organisations, policies, etc. do the most to make the world a better place."[3] Chapters 10 to 15 of this book, in discussing some of the difficulties in answering this question, convey a better idea of what is involved. They also show that the field is still very much in its infancy. That may be because it is very difficult, some say impossible, to make much progress in it. But it is too early to say how difficult it really is to make progress in prioritizing causes.

Prioritization research is just one example of a largely unexplored research area that offers the possibility of important outcomes. And it is one that is particularly likely to come to mind among people interested in effective altruism. There must be many other neglected research opportunities where the chances of making a valuable breakthrough are good enough to make a career in those areas a chance well worth taking. The problem is to find them, and that task is itself a form of prioritization research within the subcategory of research careers.

Organizers and Campaigners

People with special talents and lots of determination may be able to maximize their positive impact on the world by starting an organization. Unlike getting a job with an existing organization, where the impact you have is only the marginal difference between what you can accomplish and what the next person in line for the job would have accomplished, there are situations in which if one particular person had not started a novel organization, none of the benefits brought about by the organization would have been achieved. I have already mentioned the work of the GiveWell founders Elie Hassenfeld and Holden Karnofsky, which made being an effective altruist so much easier. Something similar can be said of what Toby Ord and Will MacAskill did by founding Giving What We Can and 80,000 Hours. Here are some other examples that show how much an individual can achieve.

Janina Ochojska grew up in Poland during the communist period. She had polio and underwent several operations as a child, but when she was a student her physical condition was so bad that no Polish doctor was prepared to operate on her again. Help came from France, where she spent a year. When she returned to Poland, she cofounded the Polish EquiLibre Foundation, modeled on a French charitable organization. Initially it assisted people in poverty in Poland, but when the war in Bosnia broke out in 1992 Janina organized an aid convoy to the beleaguered city of Sarajevo. At this time Poland was a relatively poor country, slowly recovering from more than forty years of communist rule. Ochojska became convinced that although Poles were generally poor, they were ready to help people in still greater need. She broke away from EquiLibre and established Polish Humanitarian Action, or PAH. Under her leadership, PAH organized the first Polish aid mission in Kosovo and then gradually expanded its reach to Chechnya, Iraq, Iran, Lebanon, Sri Lanka, Afghanistan, South Sudan, Somalia, the Palestinian National Authority, the Philippines, and Haiti. For this, predictably, she was asked why she was sending convoys to distant countries when there were Poles so poor that they had to rummage through the garbage to find something to eat. Ochojska's reply was to reject the idea that caring for people far away is in conflict with caring for people nearby; she believes that making people aware of the needs of others anywhere in the world will make them more aware of the needs of local people as well.[4] In accordance with this belief, PAH runs educational programs in Polish schools to make students more aware of the needs of people in developing countries. PAH also helps to integrate refugees in Polish society and lobbies the Polish government on issues affecting the global poor. Twenty years after its foundation, PAH is the leading nongovernmental Polish provider of development assistance and humanitarian relief, with annual revenues equivalent to more than US$5 million.[5]

Dharma Master Cheng Yen is a Buddhist nun living in Hualien County, a mountainous region on the east coast of Taiwan. Because the mountains formed barriers to travel, the area has a high proportion of indigenous people, and in the 1960s many people in the area, especially indigenous people, were living in poverty. Although Buddhism is sometimes regarded as promoting a retreat from the world to focus on the inner life, Cheng Yen took the opposite path. In 1966, when Cheng Yen was twenty-nine, she saw an indigenous woman with labor complications whose family had carried her for eight hours from their mountain village to Hualien City. On arriving they were told they would have to pay for the medical treatment she needed. Unable to afford the cost of treatment they had no alternative but to carry her back again. In response, Cheng Yen organized a group of thirty housewives, each of whom put aside a few cents each day to establish a charity fund for needy families. It was called Tzu

Chi, which means "Compassionate Relief." Gradually word spread, and more people joined.[6] Cheng Yen began to raise funds for a hospital in Hualien City. The hospital opened in 1986. Since then, Tzu Chi has established six more hospitals.

To train some of the local people to work in the hospital, Tzu Chi founded medical and nursing schools. Perhaps the most remarkable feature of its medical schools is the attitude shown to corpses that are used for medical purposes, such as teaching anatomy or simulation surgery, or for research. Obtaining corpses for this purpose is normally a problem in Chinese cultures because of a Confucian tradition that the body of a deceased person should be cremated with the body intact. Cheng Yen asked her volunteers to help by willing their bodies to the medical school after their death. In contrast to most medical schools, here the bodies are treated with the utmost respect for the person whose body it was. The students visit the family of the deceased and learn about his or her life. They refer to the deceased as "silent mentors," place photographs of the living person on the walls of the medical school, and have a shrine to each donor. After the course has concluded and the body has served its purpose, all parts are replaced and the body is sewn up. The medical school then arranges a cremation ceremony in which students and the family take part.

Tzu Chi is now a huge organization, with seven million members in Taiwan alone—almost 30 percent of the population—and another three million members associated with chapters in 51 countries. This gives it a vast capacity to help. After a major earthquake hit Taiwan in 1999, Tzu Chi rebuilt 51 schools. Since then it has done the same after disasters in other countries, rebuilding 182 schools in 16 countries. Tzu Chi promotes sustainability in everything it does. It has become a major recycler, using its volunteers to gather plastic bottles and other recyclables that are turned into carpets and clothing. In order to promote sustainable living as well as compassion for sentient beings all meals served in Tzu Chi hospitals, schools, universities, and other institutions are vegetarian.

From the perspective of an effective altruist, Tzu Chi does some surprising things. After the earthquake and tsunami that hit Japan in 2011, Tzu Chi raised funds to distribute hot meals to survivors, and in the wake of Hurricane Sandy, which battered New York and New Jersey in 2012, Tzu Chi distributed $10 million dollars worth of Visa debit cards, with $600 on each card, to victims of the storm.[7] When I visited the Tzu Chi hospital in Hualien, I asked Rey-Sheng Her, a spokesman for Tzu Chi, why the organization would give aid to the citizens of wealthy countries like Japan and the United States, when the money could do much more good if used to help people in extreme poverty. His answer was that it is important for Tzu Chi to show compassion and love for all, rich and poor. More practically, he suggested, it could also help to promote the work of Tzu Chi and its ideals of compassion in affluent countries.

Tzu Chi is unlikely to ever become one of GiveWell's recommended charities because it is more interested in spreading love and compassion than in demonstrating that it is getting the most good out of each dollar it spends. It has, however, inspired millions of people to show compassion to others. Behind that inspiration lies the power of the example of one woman's decision to act to help others. There can be no doubt that Cheng Yen has used her life to do an extraordinary amount of good. She continues to live austerely at a monastery near Hualien City, eschewing even the luxury of air-conditioning, despite the region's hot, humid summers. While Tzu Chi does humanitarian work in eighty-seven countries, Cheng Yen has never been outside of Taiwan.

In 2012 GiveWell ranked GiveDirectly among its top three recommended charities, a remarkable achievement given that only three years earlier the organization was no more than an idea in the heads of four graduate students studying for degrees in international development at Harvard and MIT. Michael Faye, Paul Niehaus, Jeremy Shapiro, and Rohit Wanchoo were all focused on understanding what works and what doesn't work in development. They were also trying to decide where best to send their own charitable donations. On the one hand, they had their doubts about some of the work done by traditional charities; on the other hand, they had studied the impacts of several government programs in developing countries that had simply given cash to poor people, and they knew there was strong evidence that the recipients were generally using the money responsibly, with outcomes ranging from increased earnings to improved health and more education for children. They also learned that, thanks to improved payments technology, it was possible for the first time to send money electronically to the extreme poor. The idea of using that technology to put almost all of one's donations directly into the hands of some of the world's poorest people excited them. They looked for an organization ready to take their money and use the new technology to pass it on directly to people in extreme poverty; but the organizations they talked to didn't have any plans to involve donors in direct giving. Faye, Niehaus, Shapiro, and Wanchoo suspected that such reluctance stemmed from the fear that direct giving would be a major threat to the status quo. That raised the possibility that a new organization was needed, one that did not have an interest in preserving a top-heavy infrastructure.

The group considered that cash transfers had the potential to be not just an effective way to give but also a powerful benchmark for the rest of the sector. If donors had the option of giving their money directly to the poor, then traditional organizations would face more pressure to show that they were creating so much more value for the poor that it justified the additional costs involved—for example, spending thousands of dollars to deliver a cow. The impact of giving directly could thus go beyond the direct impact of the dollars themselves. Moreover, a direct giving option would eliminate one of the most common rationales for not giving, namely, the fear that money never really gets to the people who need it. These ideas seemed important enough for the group to do something it had not anticipated doing: create a brand-new charity.

GiveDirectly started as a private giving circle in 2009 and began seeking public donations in 2011. Faye, Niehaus, Shapiro, and Wanchoo have tried to run it like the nonprofit they had wanted to give to in their graduate school days. GiveDirectly is clear and specific about what it does with money and conducts rigorous, transparent research to document the impacts of its transfers. The founders worked with independent researchers to conduct a randomized controlled trial and preannounced the study in order to tie their hands and make sure they couldn't hide any failures. Their vision for the future is to establish cash transfers as the benchmark that donors use to evaluate whether other, more traditional approaches are worth what they cost.[8]

I first met Henry Spira in 1974, when he attended an adult education course on animal liberation that I taught at New York University. He had spent most of his life working for the weak and oppressed, taking part in civil rights marches in the American South, teaching black and Hispanic kids in New York's public school system, and, while working as a merchant seaman, supporting a union reform group that took on a corrupt union boss. Then a friend going overseas dumped a cat on Henry. It had never occurred to him that nonhuman animals might be included among the weak and oppressed, but the cat prepared him to be receptive to my first essay on animal liberation, which appeared around that time.[9] He heard about the course, came to all the sessions, and at the end of it stood up and asked people if they wanted to continue to meet, not to discuss more philosophy but to see what could be done about the animal suffering we had been discussing. Eight people from the class accepted that invitation, and from that group developed the first American animal rights campaign to succeed in stopping a series of cruel and unnecessary experiments on animals. Henry went on to lead further successful campaigns, including one that persuaded cosmetic industry giants like Revlon and Avon to cease testing their products on animals. Henry's work has spared untold millions of animals acute pain and prolonged suffering. Although Henry died in 1998, his tactics have been adopted by other organizations, and his influence lives on.[10]

A Wide-Open Choice

The answer to the question, What career should I follow in order to do the most good? will depend on your interests, talents, and character. Starting a new organization can, as we have just seen, do an immense amount of good. But one also has to consider the expected value of such a choice. The odds are slim that you will do as much good as Janina Ochojska, Cheng Yen, the founders of GiveDirectly, or Henry Spira. All I have been able to do, in this chapter and the previous one, is outline a few possibilities that are worth considering if you want to maximize the amount of good you do over your lifetime.

6

Giving a Part of Yourself

In January 2013 I received an email that began as follows: "In *The Life You Can Save*, you remark that as far as you know no student of yours has ever actually donated a kidney. Last Tuesday, I bit the utilitarian bullet: I anonymously donated my right kidney to whoever could use it the most. By doing so, I started a 'kidney chain' that allowed a total of four people to receive kidneys. The idea of donating a kidney popped into my head in an Ethics class." The writer was Chris Croy, a student at St. Louis Community College, in Meramec, Missouri. He went on to tell me that although he had never taken a class with me, my writings on humans' moral obligations to others had played a role in his decision to donate his kidney. After reading my article "Famine, Affluence and Morality," Croy continued, the class had considered a counterargument by John Arthur that contained the following passage: "One obvious means by which you could aid others is with your body. Many of your extra organs (eye, kidney) could be given to another with the result that there is more good than if you kept both. You wouldn't see as well or live as long, perhaps, but that is not of comparable significance to the benefit others would receive. Yet surely the fact that it is your eye and you need it is not insignificant. Perhaps there could be cases where one is obligated to sacrifice one's health or sight, but what seems clear is that this is not true in every case where (slightly) more good would come of your doing so."[1]

Another student in the class said that we need both of our kidneys to live, but Chris knew that that was wrong and replied that donating a kidney has little to no effect on one's health and thus is actually an insignificant sacrifice. Then he spent the rest of the class thinking about what he had said. He read everything he could find about kidney donation. When his friend Chelsea told him that she was thinking of donating a kidney, the idea suddenly didn't seem so crazy. He decided to do it, and after building up his courage called the hospital. Chelsea did the same, but a scan showed that she had polycystic kidney disease, so her offer to donate was rejected. Chris went ahead on his own. More than a year after the donation, Chris was doing fine. One morning he got a call from an unfamiliar number, and a voice said, "Hello, it's your kidney calling." The kidney was now working for a forty-three-year-old schoolteacher at a school that mostly serves poor children.[2] Chris felt good about that.

Alexander Berger also made a life-changing decision after taking an ethics class, in his case at Stanford University, where he read some of my work and heard about Zell Kravinsky's donation. "At first it sounded a little bit crazy," he said, "and not something I identified with at all." But he did some research that showed that donating a kidney is a relatively safe procedure and that the benefits for the recipient are very large. In 2014 the waiting list for kidneys in the United States reached the dismal milestone of one hundred thousand, and it continues to grow. The waiting list for a deceased donor can be five years, and in some states is closer to ten years. On average, fourteen people on the waiting list die each day; some of them would have died even if they had received a kidney, so the number of lives lost because of the shortage of kidneys is less, but it is still substantial. Most people on the list are on dialysis and have a diminished life expectancy. Receiving a kidney transplant adds, on average, about ten years of life as well as greatly improving the recipient's quality of life.[3]

On the basis of the information Alexander gathered, he began to see donating a kidney as something he could do. When he told his friends and family what he was thinking of doing, they thought it was a crazy act of self-sacrifice. He insisted that it was "one of the many ways a reasonably altruistic person can help others." At the age of twenty-one he made his donation, which started a chain of six donations.[4] (These chains overcome the problem that arises when someone wants to donate to a loved one but is not a good match. A would donate to B, but cannot; C would donate to D, but cannot. If A could donate to D and C could donate to B, then it would be easy to organize an exchange, but if that is not possible, then the willingness of an altruistic donor to donate to anyone who needs a kidney can get the chain started.) Alexander is an effective altruist in other areas of his life too. He works for GiveWell, so his professional occupation is helping to find demonstrably effective charities. He also donates about 15–20 percent of his income to these charities.

Chris Croy also has an interest in effective altruism that goes beyond his kidney donation. He has become a vegan, on ethical grounds, but because his aim is to reduce suffering, he is the kind of vegan who doesn't regard avoiding trace amounts of dairy or egg in his food as being a worthwhile use of his time—in fact, he thinks that trying to be very strict about these things discourages people from becoming vegan and so causes more suffering than it prevents. As a student, he doesn't have money to donate as yet, but he is planning to do that. In fact his email went on to make a surprising comparison between donating a kidney and donating money:

I don't think what I did was all that good. A kidney transplant from a living donor usually only lasts about 25 years.
Even if you give me credit for the entire chain on the logic
that the chain could not have happened without me, we're
still only talking about 100 years, or one and a half human
lives. GiveWell.org says it costs about $2500 to save a human
life, so as far as I'm concerned giving $5000 to anti-malaria
efforts is a greater deed than giving four people kidneys.
Absolutely no-one I've explained this to has agreed with me.
What do you think?

Either way, I'm only 24, so I've got plenty of time to do
things that are *actually* really good.

I give a lot more than $5,000 each year, but I still have two kid-
neys. Going into hospital to have surgery that does no good to you
and carries a risk of harm, however small, in order to benefit a
stranger seems to me to take altruism to a very high level. It is therefore especially impressive that the number of people willing to do it,
though still relatively small, is increasing.

Along with donations of blood and bone marrow, which are now
routine procedures for saving the lives of patients, nondirected organ
donation, as it is officially called, demonstrates the existence of altruism
in a considerable section of the population, and it is a form of altruism
for which you do not need to have money. More than six million people have registered on the U.S. National Marrow Donor Program, and
there are about eleven million on donor registries worldwide.[5] Bone
marrow donation requires anesthesia and leaves the donor feeling sore
for a day or two, but there is now an alternative procedure for harvest-
ing stem cells from the blood that does not require anesthesia and in the
majority of cases serves the same function as bone marrow donation.

Blood, bone marrow, and stem cell donations are relatively simple forms of effective altruism, and as the cells soon regenerate, they can become a regular part of an altruistic life. The donation of a non-regenerative organ has long been regarded very differently. As recently as 2001, altruistic kidney donation was so rare that an article in the journal *Transplantation* argued against the "assumption of psychopathology" with which hospital staff greet people who offer to donate an organ to a stranger. On the contrary, the authors found it necessary to say, "Caring can be motivated by genuine compassion and need not be manipulatively self-serving, or born of psychopathology."[6] In 2003, when Zell Kravinsky donated a kidney to a stranger, he still had to persuade the hospital that he was serious. Radi Zaki, the director of the Centre for Renal Disease at the Albert Einstein Medical Center, in Philadelphia, said, "We made the process hard for him. We delayed, we put him off. The more impatient he got, the more delay I gave him. You want to make sure this is the real deal."[7]

Now attitudes are changing. The U.S. Organ Procurement and Transplantation Network, which is administered by the United Network for Organ Sharing, has, since 1988, kept figures on donations from living "unrelated, anonymous donors." Over the first ten years the grand total of such donations was 1. In 1998 there were 3, in 1999, 6, and in 2000, 21. The trend continued predominantly upward, passing 100 in 2008. In 2013, the last year for which information is available at the time of writing, there were 174 such donations, and a total of 1,490 organs had been donated anonymously since record keeping began.[8]

In the United Kingdom altruistic kidney donation was illegal until 2006. If you wanted to donate to someone who was not a relative, you had to apply to the Unrelated Living Transplants Regulatory Authority. As one member of that authority has written, "Our remit was precisely to reassure ourselves that there was 'something in it' for the donor. . . . [I]f we couldn't see what the donor would gain from the activity, we had to consider the 'sincerity' of their motives and occasionally had to conclude that they were being unduly pressured into donation."[9] In the first two years after altruistic organ donation became legal, 25 people volunteered to donate a kidney to a stranger, a figure that a spokesperson for the Human Tissue Authority said at the time was "remarkable."[10] The numbers have continued to grow, reaching 117 in 2013, which, given that the population in the United Kingdom is only one-fifth that of the United States, indicates that the proportion of people who donate a kidney to a stranger in Britain is three times higher than in the United States.[11]

PART THREE
MOTIVATION AND JUSTIFICATION

7

Is Love All We Need?

We now have some sense of what effective altruists do. In brief, they are sufficiently concerned about the welfare of others to make meaningful changes in their lives. Effective altruists donate to charities that, instead of making an emotional appeal to prospective donors, can demonstrate that they will use donations to save lives and reduce suffering in a way that is highly cost-effective. In order to be able to do more good, effective altruists limit their spending or take a different career path so that they will have more to give or will be more useful in some other way. They may also donate blood, stem cells, bone marrow, or a kidney to a stranger.

What motivates them? Obviously it is not conformity to social norms. The people we have met are distinctive precisely because they go beyond—in some cases, far beyond—social norms. Perhaps the first answer that comes to mind is that effective altruists are motivated by the kind of universal love we hear about so often, when people say, "All we need is love" or declare that our fellow humans are our brothers and sisters. Is it plausible that effective altruists are moved by universal love?

David Hume, that shrewd eighteenth-century observer of his fellow humans, wrote, "There is no such passion in human minds as the love of mankind, merely as such, independent of personal qualities, of services, or of relation to oneself."[1] More than a century later

Darwin's understanding of human evolution gave a scientific underpinning to Hume's observation. We now know that we are the product of a long process of genetic selection that eliminated those unable to survive, reproduce, and have surviving offspring. Love of those with a "relation to oneself," that is, our kin, is easily explained by our understanding of evolution because it promotes the survival of genes like ours. Love toward those with whom we are in a cooperative relationship or who, in Hume's language, provide us with "services" is explicable because such relationships benefit those who are involved in them. The evolutionary process would, however, seem likely to eliminate those who love and assist all humans as much as they love and assist their kin and those with whom they are in a mutually beneficial relationship.

Frans de Waal, who has spent a lifetime observing the social behavior of our closest nonhuman relatives, points out that morality probably evolved within groups, together with other related capacities for resolving conflicts, cooperating, and sharing. Yet this notion does not lead to the kind of universal altruism that effective altruists practice. On the contrary, de Waal writes, "Universally, humans treat outsiders far worse than members of their own community: in fact, moral rules hardly seem to apply to the outside."[2] Two other strong advocates of group selection as a key factor in the evolution of altruism, Elliott Sober and David Sloan Wilson, make the same point: "Group selection favors within-group niceness and between-group nastiness."[3]

Perhaps it is not love that motivates effective altruists but empathy, the ability to put oneself in the position of others and identify with their feelings or emotions. Writers like de Waal and Jeremy Rifkin have seized on the idea of empathy as, to use de Waal's words, "the grand theme of our time."[4] Rifkin believes that civilization has spread the reach of empathy beyond the family and the community so that it covers all of humankind.[5] Barack Obama has said we should talk more about "our empathy deficit."[6] Shortly after he was elected president of the United States, Obama received a letter from a young girl suggesting a ban on unnecessary wars. In response he told the girl, "If you don't already know what it means, I want you to look up the word 'empathy' in the dictionary. I believe we don't have enough empathy in our world today, and it is up to your generation to change that."[7]

If the girl followed Obama's advice and happened to use the Oxford online dictionary, she would have found *empathy* defined as follows: "The ability to understand and share the feelings of another." The distinction between understanding feelings and sharing them is important. A test used by psychologists to assess empathy, the Interpersonal Reactivity Inventory, measures four distinct components:

1. *Empathic concern* is the tendency to experience feelings of warmth, compassion, and concern for other people;
2. *Personal distress* is one's own feelings of personal unease and discomfort in reaction to the emotions of others;
3. *Perspective taking* is the tendency to adopt the point of view of other people; and
4. *Fantasy* is the tendency to imagine oneself experiencing the feelings and performing the actions of fictitious characters.

The first two refer to what one feels about others and are therefore aspects of emotional empathy. The other two are cognitive aspects of empathy. They involve knowing what something is like for another being.[8]

Emotional empathy is, in most situations, a good thing, but it is usually at its strongest when we can identify and relate to an individual. People are more willing to donate to help hungry children if they are shown a photo of one of the children and told her name and age. Telling people that there are thousands of children in need does not produce as many positive responses.[9] We can have *cognitive* empathy with thousands of children, but it is very hard to feel *emotional* empathy for so many people whom we cannot even identify as individuals.

Effective altruism does not require the kind of strong emotional empathy that people feel for identifiable individuals and can even lead to a conclusion opposed to that to which this form of emotional empathy would lead us. In one study, people were shown a photo of a child and told her name and age. They were then informed that to save her life, she needed a new, expensive drug that would cost about $300,000 to produce, and a fund was being established in an attempt to raise this sum. They were asked to donate to the fund. Another group was shown photos of eight children, given their names and ages, and told that the same sum, $300,000, was needed to produce a drug that would save *all* of their lives. They too were asked to donate. Those shown the single child gave more than those shown the eight children, presumably because they empathized with the individual child but were unable to empathize with the larger number of children.[10] To effective altruists, this is an absurd outcome, and if emotional empathy is responsible for it, then so much the worse for that kind of empathy. Effective altruists are sensitive to numbers and to cost per life saved or year of suffering prevented. If they have $10,000 to donate, they would rather give it to a charity that can save a life for $2,000 than one that can save a life for $5,000 because they would rather save five lives than two.

Do you think like the people in that study? Paul Bloom, a professor of psychology at Yale University, has suggested that if we think about our own responses, most of us will realize that we do. Imagine that you learn of an earthquake or hurricane in a remote part of the world and are told that the death toll is expected to be, say, two thousand. You feel sad about that. Later you learn that in fact twenty thousand were killed. You may feel a little worse, but it is unlikely that you feel anything like ten times worse.[11]

Effective altruists, as we have seen, need not be utilitarians, but they share a number of moral judgments with utilitarians. In particular, they agree with utilitarians that, other things being equal, we ought to do the most good we can. In a study of the role of emotion in moral decision making, subjects were presented with so-called trolley problem dilemmas in which, for example, a runaway trolley is heading for a tunnel in which there are five people, and it will kill them all unless you divert it down a sidetrack, in which case only one person will be killed. In a variant, the only way to stop the five being killed is to push a heavy stranger off a footbridge. He will be killed, but his body is heavy enough to stop the trolley and save the five. In three different experiments, those who made consistently utilitarian judgments were found to have lower levels of empathic concern than those who made nonutilitarian judgments. Empathic concern is, as we have seen, one aspect of emotional empathy. Other aspects of empathy, including personal distress and perspective taking, did not vary between those who made consistently utilitarian judgments and those who did not. Neither did demographic or cultural differences, including age, gender, education, and religiosity.[12]

Another trolley problem study used virtual reality technology to give people a more vivid sense of being in the situation in which they must decide whether to throw the switch to divert the trolley down the sidetrack, thereby killing one but saving five. In this study, experimenters measured the skin conductivity of their subjects while making these decisions. The extent to which the skin conducts electricity depends on its moisture level and therefore reveals slight sweating, which is a sign of emotional arousal. Those subjects who made utilitarian decisions showed lower levels of emotional arousal.[13] If, as these two findings strongly suggest, utilitarians are less prone to feel emotional empathy than others, it seems unlikely that effective altruists are dramatically different in this regard. At the very least, their altruistic actions are not likely to be the result of *greater* emotional empathy than people who do not act altruistically.

In response to those who think that what the world most needs is an expansion of empathy, Bloom writes, "Our best hope for the future is not to get people to think of all humanity as family—that's impossible. It lies, instead, in an appreciation of the fact that, even if we don't empathize with distant strangers, their lives have the same value as the lives of those we love."[14] The effective altruists we met in the previous chapters seem to be predominantly those who appreciate the fact that the lives of distant strangers have the same value as the lives of those we love and who are sensitive to the numbers of people they can help. To say this is not to deny that they empathize with those whom they are helping but rather to say that empathy is not what distinguishes them from other, less altruistic people. Bloom, in discussing one of the studies already mentioned, makes an observation that suggests a quite different explanation of our capacity for altruism: "To the extent that we can recognize the numbers as significant, it's because of reason, not empathy."

The strongest objection to the claim that reason plays a crucial role in the motivation of effective altruists comes from Hume's influential view that reason can never initiate an action because all action starts with a passion or desire. In a famous sentence, Hume wrote, "Reason is, and ought only to be the slave of the passions." This is, in modern parlance, an instrumentalist view of reason. Reason helps us to get what we want: it cannot tell us what to want or at least not what to want for its own sake. To argue that reason plays a crucial role in the motivation of effective altruists, we have to reject this instrumentalist view of practical reason.

Against Hume's famous sentence, we can put one from Immanuel Kant: "Two things fill the mind with ever new and increasing admiration and awe, the oftener and more steadily we reflect on them: the starry heavens above me and the moral law within me."[15] For Kant the moral law is a law of reason; but Kant asserts that reflection on this law of reason gives rise to feelings. What he fails to explain, however, is how the eternal truths of reason can generate feelings in all human beings, with their distinct empirical natures. In the light of this difficulty, Hume's view may seem the only defensible one.

Henry Sidgwick, the last of the great nineteenth-century utilitarians (after Jeremy Bentham and John Stuart Mill), shared with Kant the belief that ethics has a rational basis, but he did more than Kant to make this a credible form of motivation. Sidgwick held that there are self-evident fundamental moral principles, or axioms, which we grasp through our reasoning capacity. For our purposes the most relevant of these fundamental principles are as follows:

The good of any one individual is of no more importance, from the point of view (if I may say so) of the Universe, than the good of any other; unless, that is, there are special grounds for believing that more good is likely to be realised in the one case than in the other.

To this statement Sidgwick adds another claim, this time about what a rational being is bound to aim at:

And it is evident to me that as a rational being I am bound to aim at good generally,—so far as it is attainable by my efforts,—not merely at a particular part of it.

From these two principles Sidgwick deduces what he calls "the maxim of Benevolence, in an abstract form":

Each one is morally bound to regard the good of any other individual as much as his own, except in so far as he judges it to be less, when impartially viewed, or less certainly know-able or attainable by him.[16]

This maxim—and, for that matter, the two principles that led Sidgwick to it—is very similar to the principle that Bloom proposed as a better hope for the future than the idea of extending empathy to everyone on the planet. It is also exactly the kind of principle that would guide receptive people to do the things that, as we have seen in the previous chapters, effective altruists do. Sidgwick thinks these judgments give rise to a "dictate of reason," by which he means that if we were purely rational beings, it would motivate us to action. Human beings are not purely rational beings, so although accepting the dictate of reason will give us a motive to act in the way the maxim of benevolence prescribes, we are likely to have other motives, some of which will support it and some that may conflict with it. Among the supporting motives will be what Sidgwick called "sympathy and philanthropic enthusiasm," by which he may mean something akin to what today would be called empathy. Among the opposing mo-tives may be racism, nationalism, and egoism. But in a person who sees that it is more rational to aim at the good of all than the good of some smaller group, following one's own interest and disregarding the interests of others is likely to seem "ignoble." That will produce a sense of discomfort that Sidgwick calls "the normal emotional concomitant or expression" of the recognition that the good of the whole—that is, of everyone—is to be preferred to the good of the part, that is, oneself. We like to think of ourselves as reasonable beings, and so the recognition that we are acting contrary to reason can threaten our self-respect.[17] Note that Sidgwick does not say that people who recognize the importance of acting for the good of the whole lack emotional motivation; on the contrary, he thinks their recognition of the importance of acting for the good of the whole brings about an emotional response within them. If this is right, reason can give rise to an emotion, or passion, at least in human beings for whom self-respect matters, and Hume's dictum about reason being the slave of the passions is turned on its head.

8

One Among Many

Bernard Williams argued that human beings are not the kind of creatures who can take "the point of view of the universe":

> The difficulty is . . . that the moral dispositions, and indeed other loyalties and commitments, have a certain depth or thickness; they cannot simply be regarded, least of all by their possessor, just as devices for generating actions or states of affairs. Such dispositions and commitments will characteristically be what gives one's life some meaning, and gives one some reason for living it. . . . There is simply no conceivable exercise that consists in stepping completely outside myself and from that point of view evaluating *in toto* the dispositions, projects and affections that constitute the substance of my own life.[1]

Effective altruists seem to have achieved what Williams thought cannot be done. They are able to detach themselves from more personal considerations that otherwise dominate the way in which we live. This detachment is not total, but it does make an important difference to how they live, and it is based on reasoning of a kind that comes close to evaluating how they are living from a point of view that is independent of their own "dispositions, projects and affections." Here are some commonly expressed dispositions and affections that effective altruists would consider misguided grounds for giving:

- I give to breast cancer research because my wife died of breast cancer.
- I always wanted to be an artist but never had the opportunity, so now I direct my charitable contributions to organizations that provide opportunities for promising artists to develop their creative talents.
- I am passionate about photographing nature, so I donate to protect our wonderful national parks.
- Because I am an American, disadvantaged Americans have the first call on my charity.
- I love dogs so I give to my local animal shelter.

The influence that "the point of view of the universe" has on one's behavior will vary from person to person. Perhaps it is significant that many effective altruists decided on their overall goal while they were still quite young, before they were too deeply embedded in more particular projects or, in some cases, close personal attachments to people who do not share their values. As infants we cannot reason, but we can and do have emotions about a wide range of things. When we begin to reason we are likely to use reason to generalize and draw inferences from those situations about which we already have an emotional attitude. Nevertheless, reason is no mere slave to the passions. By modifying and redirecting our passions, it can play a critical part in the process that leads us to act ethically.

The possibility that our capacity to reason can play a critical role in a decision to live ethically offers a solution to the perplexing problem that effective altruism would otherwise pose for evolutionary theory. There is no difficulty in explaining why evolution would select for a capacity to reason: that capacity enables us to solve a variety of problems, for example, to find food or suitable partners for reproduction or other forms of cooperative activity, to avoid predators, and to outwit our enemies. If our capacity to reason also enables us to see that the good of others is, from a more universal perspective, as important as our own good, then we have an explanation for why effective altruists act in accordance with such principles. Like our ability to do higher mathematics, this use of reason to recognize fundamental moral truths would be a by-product of another trait or ability that was selected for because it enhanced our reproductive fitness—something that in evolutionary theory is known as a spandrel.[2]

Further support for the hypothesis that reason can provide a crucial element of the motivation for altruism comes from what we can observe about effective altruists. When they talk about why they act as they do, they often use language that is more suggestive of a rational insight than of an emotional impulse. Zell Kravinsky, for example, told Ian Parker that the reason many people didn't understand his desire to donate a kidney is that "they don't understand math." That's not literally true, of course. What Kravinsky meant is that they did not understand that, because the risk of dying as a result of donating a kidney is only one in four thousand, not to donate a kidney to someone in need is to value one's own life at four thousand times that of a stranger, a view Zell thought was wrong. The relevance of the remark is that Zell explained the failure of others to understand his motivation in terms of a deficiency in a cognitive capacity, not of the absence of a feeling or emotion. Toby Ord made a similar comment when he explained his shift to what we would now describe as effective altruism as the outcome of his calculation about how many people he could help if he lived modestly and donated everything above that to effective charities. It then seemed obvious to him that this was what he ought to do. Celso Vieira, the Brazilian effective altruist, said that he is "more moved by arguments than by empathy." Rachel Maley, a Chicago-based pianist and multidisciplinary artist, wrote in a blog for The Life You Can Save, "Numbers turned me into an altruist. When I learned that I could spend my exorbitant monthly gym membership (I don't even want to tell you how much it cost) on curing blindness instead, the only thought I had was, 'Why haven't I been doing this all along?' That question changed my life forever. I rethought all my financial priorities. Because sentimentalism had ruled my charitable choices up to that point, Effective Altruism was like a beam of clarity."[3]

The *New York Times* columnist David Brooks recognized the intellectual basis of effective altruism—and was clearly uncomfortable with it—when he was criticizing the idea of "earning to give": "If you see the world on a strictly intellectual level, then a child in Pakistan or Zambia is just as valuable as your own child. But not many people actually think this way. Not many people value abstract life perceived as a statistic as much as the actual child being fed, hugged, nurtured and played with."[4] Critics of effective altruism often suggest, as Brooks is doing here, that there is something odd or unnatural about being moved by the "strictly intellectual" understanding that a child in Pakistan or Zambia is just as valuable as your own child.[5] But as I said in the preface, loving your own child does not mean you have to be so dazzled by your love that you are unable to see that there is a point of view from which other children matter just as much as your own or that this perspective is unable to have an impact on the way you live.

It is telling that effective altruists talk more about the number of people they are able to help than about helping particular individuals. This interest in numbers is reflected in their giving; they give to the organizations they have reason to believe will do the most good, which often means that the donation will help more people than it would if it were given to a less effective organization. Many people who give to help people in poor countries sponsor individual children, a practice that indicates their need to focus on a particular individual whom they can get to know in some way but is not likely to benefit as many people.

Consistent with the points just made, many of the most prominent effective altruists have backgrounds in or are particularly strong in areas that require abstract reasoning, like mathematics and computing. Zell Kravinsky drew on his math skills to become a successful real estate investor. Toby Ord was studying math and computer science before he went into philosophy. Matt Wage did well in math at Princeton before deciding to major in philosophy. Ian Ross studied math and computer science at MIT as an undergraduate. Jim Greenbaum's numeracy skills were always at the top of his class. Philipp Gruissem's outstanding success in poker tournaments is sufficient proof that he has a strong grasp of probabilities. Celso Vieira excels in tasks requiring analytic reasoning. My favorite example of the combination of effective altruism and numeracy is the website Counting Animals, which has the subtitle "A place for people who love animals and numbers" and a home page stating that "nerdism meets animal rights here!"

We can speculate that people with a high level of abstract reasoning ability are more likely to take the kind of approach to helping others that is characteristic of effective altruism. This speculation gains some support from research into how donors to a charity respond to information about the effectiveness of the charity. Dean

Karlan and Daniel Wood worked with Freedom from Hunger, a U.S.-based charity, to vary their fund-raising letters. The standard letter included a description of an individual who had benefited by Freedom from Hunger's work. Such descriptions, as we have seen, arouse an emotional response. To the letters sent to a random sample of donors Karlan and Wood added information giving scientific evidence of the effectiveness of Freedom from Hunger's work. They found that this information increased the number of donations received from large donors, who had previously given $100 or more, but *decreased* the number of donations received from small donors. As we noticed earlier, small donors who give to many charities tend to be "warm glow" donors who are not really concerned to do the most good. As Karlan and Wood write, "Our finding that smaller prior donors respond to information on charitable effectiveness by donating less frequently and in smaller amounts is consistent with other research showing that emotional impulses for giving shut down in the presence of analytical information."[6] Effective altruists, on the other hand, are strongly influenced by analytical information, which suggests that their emotional impulses are not inhibited by such information. Instead, they use it to override those elements of their emotional impulses that lead other people to act less effectively.

The hypothesis that effective altruists tend, to a higher degree than many other people, to allow their reasoning abilities to override and redirect their emotions is consistent with more than a decade of psychological research on Joshua Greene's suggestion that we use two distinct processes when we make moral judgments. Greene suggests that the way most people make moral judgments can be thought of as akin to taking photographs with a camera that is normally used in "point-and-shoot" mode but can be switched to a manual mode that overrides the automatic settings. When we are confronted with a situation calling for moral judgment, we usually have an instinctive gut reaction that tells us when something is wrong. Like a point-and-shoot camera, our intuitive responses are quick and easy to operate and in normal conditions yield good results; but in rare situations with special features, they can lead us astray. In that case we will do better if we switch to manual mode, in other words, put aside our instinctive reactions and think the issue through.[7]

Point-and-shoot cameras were designed to enable people who are not expert photographers to take good photographs in most circumstances. Our quick moral responses were not designed but evolved by natural selection. Given that for most of our evolutionary history we lived in small tribal groups, it is no surprise that we developed instinctive responses that led us to help our kin and those with whom we could form cooperative relationships but did not favor helping distant strangers or animals.

The most controversial aspect of this model is that it links moral judgments characteristically based on the idea that something is just wrong in itself, independently of its consequences, to the instinctive, emotionally based point-and-shoot mode of reaching a moral judgment and links characteristically utilitarian judgments to the manual mode, which draws on our conscious thought processes, or reasoning, as well as on emotional attitudes. An early piece of evidence for this view came from a study in which Greene and his colleagues asked people to make judgments about trolley problems and similar moral dilemmas while images were being taken of their brain activity. The study showed increased activity in brain areas associated with cognitive control before a subject made a utilitarian judgment but not before making a nonutilitarian judgment.[8] This suggestive finding has since been supported by a wide variety of further evidence. For example, in another study some subjects were asked, before they were presented with the moral dilemma, to memorize a string of letters, digits, and special characters, such as *n63#m1Q,* before each dilemma. They were told they would be asked to repeat the sequence after the experiment was over. This is known as cognitive loading—it puts a load on the parts of the brain associated with reasoning. When these subjects were then presented with the moral dilemmas, they were more likely than similar subjects who were not cognitively loaded to make judgments suggesting that some acts are just wrong, irrespective of their consequences. Remembering the sequence made it more difficult for them to reason adequately, and so they gave a more intuitive response. Similarly, when subjects were shown a photo of the single individual who would be harmed if they did not choose to act so as to save the larger number of individuals, they were less likely to give a utilitarian response, presumably because the photo aroused their empathy with the victim. Other studies of cognitive loading have yielded similar results.[9] Many other studies also support Greene's dual-process theory of how we make moral judgments.[10] These studies bolster as well the more specific claim that associates characteristically consequentialist judgments with greater use of conscious reasoning processes.

To avoid possible misunderstandings, I reiterate that I am not trying to paint effective altruists as coldly rational calculating machines. Holden Karnofsky, the cofounder of GiveWell, has blogged about what he sees as the misconception that effective altruists are, in order to act as rationally as possible, suppressing their passions. That, he insists, isn't the case. Instead, he writes, *"Effective altruism is what we are passionate about. We're excited by the idea of making the most of our resources and helping others as much as possible. . . . I'd have trouble sustaining interest in a cause if I felt that I could do more good by switching to another. I'm not describing how I 'should'* think or 'try to' think. I'm describing what excites me. . . . This excitement is what drove the all-nighters that started GiveWell, and I believe I couldn't be as motivated or put in as much effort on any other project."[11] Comments on Holden's blog divided between some with whom it resonated and others who thought he was giving too much ground to the critics and should be standing up for reason rather than accepting that there is something negative about the idea of following reason rather than passion. Uri Katz, a graduate student at Hebrew University in Jerusalem, asked Holden what he would do if he were to wake up one morning and find he has a passion for working in a soup kitchen and little passion for his work at GiveWell. Would he go and work at the soup kitchen, even though he would do much more good if he continued to work at GiveWell? In response Holden said he found it difficult to engage with a hypothetical question that involved such a fundamental transformation, but added, "I would have a tough decision and would have a real chance of opting for the soup kitchen." Why, though, is this even a tough decision? Why does Holden not say simply, "Yes, of course, then I would work at the soup kitchen"? Because, I suggest, reason is playing a role in his decision making, as it should.

We can see reason playing this role, in conjunction with emotion, in the work for animals undertaken by Harish Sethu, the founder of the "nerdism meets animal rights" website Counting Animals. Sethu said to me, "I find that videos of animal suffering always draw an intense emotional response in me. I am slightly embarrassed to say that they always make me cry. All the rational number crunching I do is ultimately motivated by this emotion (compassion, mercy, etc.). . . . I am moved by both emotion and reason." For Sethu, the emotional response to suffering is the ultimate motivator, but he recognizes that the suffering he is seeing on a video is part of a much larger universe of animal suffering. That recognition does not dampen his emotional response, as it does in people who are told about a group of children in need rather than one child.[12] Neither does he take his emotional response to a video of, say, an abused dog as a reason for trying to do something to help that dog or even to help dogs in general. Instead, as we shall see in chapter 13 when we consider what an effective altruist should do about animal suffering, he reasons about how he can make the biggest possible reduction in the suffering in that larger universe of suffering.

If a high level of abstract reasoning ability is conducive to effective altruism, we can ask why it has emerged as a movement only now. Have people's abstract reasoning abilities suddenly improved? Several factors are likely to be involved. In affluent nations a sizable segment of the population lives very comfortably and does not have to worry about economic security. In these circumstances, the need to find meaning and fulfillment in life comes to the fore, and many people turn to effective altruism as a way of giving their lives a purpose it would not otherwise have. Moreover, substantial wealth is now coming to a new generation of people who work in areas that analyze data and evidence. They are likely to be more ready to embrace the idea of giving based on doing the most good as opposed to giving based on family traditions, social conventions, or personal feelings. Technological changes that make it possible for effective altruists to connect with each other via the Internet have been important. The establishment of GiveWell has eased the difficulty of knowing where best to give.

These developments might well be sufficient triggers for the emergence of effective altruism, even if our reasoning abilities had remained static. Surprisingly, however, these abilities really have improved measurably in the relatively short time span of the past century. The average IQ score is still 100, but that is only because IQ test scores are standardized to produce this result. The tests themselves are changed from time to time in order to bring the raw scores closer to the standardized scores. In every major industrialized nation, raw scores have risen by an average of about 3 points per decade. The phenomenon is known as the Flynn effect, after James Flynn, who published papers on it in 1984 and 1987.[13] It has been estimated that by today's standards the average IQ in the United States in 1932 was only 80.[14]

Several explanations have been put forward for this rise in IQ scores, ranging from better nutrition to a more stimulating environment that requires us to do more thinking. Better education may have played some part, but scores have risen most on those questions that test the ability to reason abstractly rather than on the sections that test vocabulary and math. Flynn later proposed that the spread throughout the population of scientific modes of reasoning about problems could contribute to an improvement in reasoning.[15]

Steven Pinker believes that the improvement in our reasoning abilities may have begun when the development of the printing press spread ideas and information to a much larger proportion of the population. He argues that better reasoning had a positive moral impact too. We became better able to take an impartial stance and detach ourselves from our personal and parochial perspectives. Pinker calls this a "*moral* Flynn effect."[16] If he is right, this effect could have led more people to the kind of ethical views that are characteristic of effective altruism. Who knows what changes the twenty-first century, with its enormous expansion of personal communications and thus of contacts with others both near and far, will bring to human nature, to our brains, and to our moral sense?

9

Altruism and Happiness

When people learn what effective altruists have done, they often wonder what would lead someone to make so great a sacrifice for a stranger. But many effective altruists don't see what they are doing as a sacrifice at all. Holden Karnofsky touches on that in a blog post on "Excited Altruism," saying that he and Elie don't consider themselves unusually selfless or feel that they made a sacrifice in starting GiveWell. "Compared to when we worked in finance," he writes, "we find our work more interesting, more exciting, more motivating, and better for meeting people that we have strong connections with, all of which easily makes up for pay cuts that haven't much affected our lifestyles."[1] The effective altruists we met earlier do not generally see what they are doing as a sacrifice either. Toby Ord initially thought that living on £18,000 a year would be a sacrifice worth making because of the good he could do with the income he was forgoing. Later he realized that it wasn't a sacrifice at all because his sense of engagement in making the world a better place means far more to him than new gadgets or a bigger house.[2] Julia Wise, as we saw, sees her ability to save hundreds of lives as an "amazing opportunity" but demands no more of herself than she can cheerfully give. Ian Ross is familiar with psychological research about the "hedonic treadmill" of consumer spending, which shows that when we consume more, we enjoy it for a short time but then adapt to that level and need to consume still more to maintain our level of enjoyment. Hence, he says, while donating doesn't give him much of a rush, he also doesn't think he is missing out on much. Charlie Bresler, the unpaid executive director of The Life You Can Save, has told me, "I truly do not believe in 'altruism'—I believe the life I am saving is my own and that I should have started doing this kind of work much sooner!"

Too often we equate making a sacrifice with doing something that causes us to have less money. Money, however, is not an intrinsic good. Rather than saying that something is a sacrifice if it will cause you to have less money, it would be more reasonable to say that something is a sacrifice if it causes you to have a lower level of well-being or, in a word, be less happy. Therefore, to determine whether effective altruists are making a sacrifice, we need to look at the chief determinants of happiness or at least at those that might be affected by the kinds of choices that effective altruists make. Recent psychological research shows that in this respect Holden, Toby, Julia, and Ian are not unusual. Studies of the relationship between income and happiness or well-being indicate that for people at low levels of income, an increase in income does lead to greater happiness, but once income is sufficient to provide for one's needs and a degree of financial security, further increases have either much less impact on happiness or no impact at all. Other things, especially warm personal relationships, contribute much more. One study calculated that for single people earning their society's median income, finding a domestic partner would give as big a boost to happiness as a 767 percent increase in income.[3]

Two groups of researchers have asked samples of Americans to estimate the happiness of people on low incomes. In one study, respondents were asked to estimate how much time people living on less than $20,000 a year spent in a bad mood; the other study sought opinions on the happiness of people earning $55,000 and below. Both studies had data that answered the questions they were asking their samples to estimate. The former study found the estimated prevalence of bad mood was "grossly exaggerated," and the latter found that people "vastly underestimated" how happy people at the specified relatively low incomes were likely to be.[4]

Perhaps we imagine that money is important to our well-being because we need money to buy consumer goods, and buying things has become an obsession that beckons us away from what really advances our well-being. An in-depth study of thirty-two families in Los Angeles found that three-quarters of them could not park their cars in their garages because the garages were too full of stuff. The volume of possessions was so great that managing them elevated levels of stress hormones in mothers.[5] Despite the fact that the growth in size of the typical American home means that Americans today have three times the amount of space, per person, that they had in 1950, they still pay a total of $22 billion a year to rent extra storage space.[6] Are they happier for having so much stuff? Graham Hill has known both sides of this question. After selling an Internet consulting company, he bought a four-story 3,600-square-foot house and filled it with all the latest consumer goods. His enjoyment was brief; he soon became numb to his possessions and found that his life had become much more complicated. He now lives in a 420-square-foot apartment with a minimum of possessions and likes his life far better than before.[7]

Although using our income to buy more stuff does not make us happier, it turns out that using it to help others does. Elizabeth Dunn, Lara Aknin, and Michael Norton gave a sum of money to participants in an experiment, instructing half of them to spend it on themselves and the other half to buy a present for someone or donate it to charity. At the end of the day, those who spent the money on others were happier than those who spent it on themselves.[8] This result is in line with Gallup survey data. People in 136 countries were asked, "Have you donated money to charity in the last month?" They were also asked to rate, on a ten-point scale, how happy they are. In 122 of the 136 countries there was a positive correlation between having donated to charity in the past month and being at a higher level of happiness. The difference in the level of reported happiness between those who answered yes to the question about donating to charity and those who answered no was equivalent to the difference made by a doubling of income.[9]

The survey shows a correlation, not causation, and it seems that the causation can run both ways because people who are happy are more likely to give to help others.[10] This observation led Aknin, Dunn, and Norton to ask whether recalling an act of spending to help others leads to an increase in happiness and whether this increase in turn makes people more likely to spend on others in the near future. They were able to show that there is a reciprocal relation between the two, producing a positive feedback loop that leads to more spending on others and greater happiness. The authors write that their findings might "have implications for individuals seeking to escape the hedonic treadmill" and offer "a path to sustainable happiness."[11]

Many people accept the notion that money can't buy happiness and therefore that for people living in affluent countries on average or above-average incomes, giving money can bring benefits that outweigh the loss of spending power. But what of donating a part of one's body? Having surgery, taking time off to recover, and accepting a degree of risk to one's long-term health and longevity, all for a complete stranger—even if the risk is small, isn't that still a sacrifice? Again, the evidence says it is not. In one study, seven people who gave nondirected organ donations (six kidney donors and one who donated a liver segment) were interviewed three months after the donation. Three of them had met the recipients of their donations and found this a satisfying experience. The other four had chosen to remain anonymous, but all said they were pleased with what they had done. None experienced psychological problems. According to the authors of the study, "On a scale of 1–10, with 10 being best, an average score of 9.8 was given in rating the overall donation experience while an average score of 10 was given to willingness to do it over again."[12] Sue Rabbitt Roff, who was a lay member of the Unrelated Live Transplant Regulatory Authority in the United Kingdom, reports that "every study of live kidney donors from Turkey to Scotland has reported enhanced self-esteem among the donors."[13] If many kidney donors had to deal with major health problems because of their donation, then the enhancement to their self-esteem might be outweighed by the worse health outcome, but such health issues are, fortunately, very rare.[14]

Self-esteem is an important component of happiness.[15] The Canadian philosopher Richard Keshen has developed a concept of reasonable self-esteem that fits particularly well with the mindset of effective altruists, given that, as we have seen, many of them rely more on their reasoning capacities than on their emotions. Keshen begins with the concept of a reasonable person—that is, a person whose defining commitment is to have reasonable beliefs about the world, about what is in her interests, and about what she ought to do.[16] A reasonable person seeks to hold beliefs that are in accord with the relevant evidence and values that are not open to reasonable criticism by others. Here Keshen anticipates Thomas Scanlon's idea of sound ethical decisions as those that others cannot reasonably reject.[17] Granted, all this leaves open what values are reasonable, but at a minimum reasonable values are values that are not influenced by biased thinking and hence can be defended to others. To be a reasonable person is to be part of a long line of thinkers, stretching back to Aristotle, who appealed to reason and argument rather than to authority or faith. To the reasonable person, self-esteem must be based on evidence and reasonable values.

At the core of the reasonable person's ethical life, according to Keshen, is a recognition that others are like us and therefore, in some sense, their lives and their well-being matter as much as our own. Therefore the reasonable person cannot have self-esteem while ignoring the interests of others whose well-being she recognizes as being equally significant. The most solid basis for self-esteem is to live an ethical life, that is, a life in which one contributes to the greatest possible extent to making the world a better place. Doing this is not, therefore, altruism in a sense that involves giving up what one would rather be doing, nor does it involve alienation or a loss of integrity, as Bernard Williams claimed. It is, on the contrary, the expression of the core of one's identity. When Henry Spira, the pioneering campaigner for animals whom we met in chapter 5, knew he did not have long to live, he said to me, "When I go, I want to look back and say: 'I made this world a better place for others.' But it's not a sense of duty, rather, this is what I want to do. I feel best when I'm doing it well."[18]

If, as I have just argued, effective altruists are not making a sacrifice, do they deserve to be considered altruists at all? The idea of altruism always has in it the idea of concern for others, but beyond that, understandings can differ. Some interpretations imply a complete denial of one's own interests in order to serve others. On this view, if the rich man were to do as Jesus told him—to sell all he has and give the proceeds to the poor—he would still not be an altruist because he was asking Jesus what he must do to inherit eternal life. Similarly, on a Buddhist view, helping others and protecting life advances one's own well-being too. If one can, through virtuous living and meditation, achieve enlightenment, one transcends one's ego and knows the sufferings and joys of every sentient being. There is no sense of loss in this transcendence of the quest to satisfy desires that previously seemed so important or of the pleasures that came from their satisfaction, for enlightenment involves detachment from one's desires.[19]

We do not have to make self-sacrifice a necessary element of altruism. We can regard people as altruists because of the kind of interests they have rather than because they are sacrificing their interests. A story told about the seventeenth-century philosopher Thomas Hobbes illustrates this point. During his lifetime, Hobbes was notorious because his philosophy was based on egoism, the idea that people always do what is in their interests. One day while walking through London he gave alms to a beggar. A companion immediately accused him of refuting his own theory. Hobbes replied that it pleased him to see the beggar made happy, so his gift was consistent with egoism. But now imagine that Hobbes did this all day, every day; that he actively sought out people in need and offered them assistance, to a point at which he reduced his fortune and lived more simply so that he could give more. He continues to explain his actions by saying that his greatest joy comes from seeing people made happier.

Is this imaginary Hobbes an egoist? If so, the claim that we are all egoists has been weakened to the point that it no longer shocks. On this understanding of egoism, the apparent dichotomy between egoism and altruism ceases to matter. What is really of import is the concern people have for the interests of others. If we want to encourage people to do the most good, we should not focus on whether what they are doing involves a sacrifice, in the sense that it makes them less happy. We should instead focus on whether what makes them happy involves increasing the well-being of others. If we wish, we can redefine the terms *egoism* and *altruism* in this way, so that they refer to whether people's interests include a strong concern for others—it if does, then let's call them altruists, whether or not acting on this concern for others involves a gain or loss for the "altruist."

PART FOUR
CHOOSING CAUSES AND ORGANIZATIONS

10

Domestic or Global?

Trying to do the most good involves making difficult judgments, not only about which charities are most highly effective but also about the broad areas in which our resources will do the most good. So far I have taken aiding the world's poorest people as my leading example of a highly effective cause; but is it the *most* effective possible cause? How does it compare with efforts to stop the infliction of suffering on animals? to mitigate the damage we are doing to the climate of our planet? to save endangered species from extinction? or perhaps to save ourselves, by reducing the risk that we will wipe ourselves out?

The field of philanthropy has, as a whole, been extremely reluctant to tackle these comparative questions. That may be because finding the answers involves not only questions of fact that are difficult to establish but also controversial value judgments. To assume that there is no point in even trying to answer them and that all philanthropic causes are alike is a common error, but one with very serious consequences in terms of missed opportunities to do more good. One large, influential organization that has made this mistake is Rockefeller Philanthropy Advisors. We can take it as an example of the error not because in this respect it is any worse than many other philanthropic advisors but because it is one of the world's largest philanthropic service organizations. It claims to have advised a total of more than $3 billion in charitable giving and to advise an additional $200 million each year.

The Rockefeller Philanthropy Advisors website features a series of leaflets called "Your Philanthropy Roadmap." The goal of the series is stated to be helping donors create "thoughtful, effective giving programs." One leaflet, "Finding Your Focus in Philanthropy," includes a chart showing various areas in which a philanthropist might give: health and safety, education, arts, culture and heritage, human and civil rights, economic security, and environment.[1]

Curiously, this set of categories allows no place for animal welfare, although as we shall see in chapter 13 that field offers opportunities for greatly reducing suffering at modest cost. Animal welfare does not fit into the environment category because much of the suffering humans inflict on animals takes place in factory farms, laboratories, puppy mills, zoos, and circuses. Although these places, especially the factory farms, do have a negative environmental impact, that is distinct from their impact on animal suffering.

The way in which Rockefeller Philanthropy Advisors divides up the field of philanthropy also fails to indicate that intending donors living in affluent countries must choose whether to give to an organization that acts domestically or one with a focus beyond their country's borders. That choice determines whether they will benefit people who are already among the wealthiest one-third of the world or those who are far worse off. In the Rockefeller list, giving to reduce global poverty does not even appear as a category—presumably it is divided among health and safety, economic security, and environment—but one could reasonably see the decision whether to give to health or economic security as less significant than the decision whether to give to projects in the United States or in some of the world's poorest countries.

Among the various philanthropic projects the leaflet describes are one seeking to improve health care for the global poor and another aimed at improving health care in the United States:

- In 1998 Ted Turner gave a billion dollars, or a third of his wealth, to the UN to scale up proven health programs focused on the world's biggest killer diseases, which overwhelmingly kill children in developing countries.

This initiative has been highly successful, drawing in and coordinating funds from other nonprofits, such as the Gates Foundation. Since 2000, 1.1 billion children have been given a combined vaccine that prevents measles and rubella. The vaccine now reaches 84 percent of the world's children. Between 2000 and 2012, worldwide deaths from measles have fallen 78 percent, with a total of 13.8 million deaths averted.[2] The cost per vaccination is estimated to be $1. If that figure is correct, the estimated cost per life saved would be just under $80.[3]

- In 1986 Lucile Packard gave a $40 million donation to establish a hospital in Palo Alto, California, and established a foundation to give further ongoing support.

The Lucile Packard Children's Hospital in Palo Alto has been in the news for its success in achieving difficult separations of conjoined twins. For example, in 2007 the hospital separated two girls from Costa Rica who shared a liver. The operation took nine hours and involved twenty-two people at a cost estimated at somewhere between $1 million and $2 million. One of the girls then needed open heart surgery for a congenital heart defect, and the other also needed another operation to reconstruct her chest cavity. Follow-up operations on each girl were also required. The hospital paid for the operations, and the doctors donated their time, while the family's travel and stay in the United States—which lasted about six months before the girls were well enough to go back to Costa Rica—was assisted by a charity called Mending Kids International.

In 2012 Palo Alto was ranked by CNN as the third wealthiest town in the United States, with a median family income of $163, 661.[4]

What Rockefeller Philanthropy Advisors does not say, in describing these two projects, is that the cost of saving a child's life in an intensive care hospital in the United States is typically thousands of times higher than the cost of saving the life of a child in a developing country. Such disparities are not limited to rare cases like the separation of conjoined twins. Intensive care for a newborn in the United States costs around $3,500 per day, and for a prolonged stay it is not unusual for costs to exceed $1 million.[5] It doesn't seem all that difficult to judge that it is better to use a million dollars to save the lives of hundreds of children by protecting them from measles than to use it to separate one pair of conjoined twins or save one extremely premature infant.[6] Governments arguably have the responsibility to look after their own citizens first, but individuals have no such responsibility.

Toby Ord has given another example of the cost differences between helping people in affluent countries and helping people elsewhere. You may have received appeals for donations from charities in affluent countries that provide blind people with guide dogs. That sounds like a cause worthy of support—until you consider the costs and the alternatives to which you could donate. It costs about $40,000 to supply one person in the United States with a guide dog;

most of the expense is incurred in training the dog and the recipient. But the cost of preventing someone from going blind because of trachoma, the most common cause of preventable blindness, is in the range of $20–$100. If you do the math, you will see the choice we face is to provide one person with a guide dog or prevent anywhere between four hundred and two thousand cases of blindness in developing countries.[7]

When I suggest to audiences in the United States that we should help the world's poorest people, a very common response is that we should help the poor in our own country first. Poverty in the United States, however, is very different from poverty in developing countries. So different, in fact, that even those who think it defensible to give some degree of priority to helping our compatriots might, when fully informed of the difference, be led to reconsider whether it is right to discount the lives and interests of people beyond the borders of our country so heavily that assisting the poor in an affluent country like the United States should take priority over assisting some of the world's poorest people. In 2012 the U.S. government poverty threshold for a family of four was $23,850.[8] That works out to a per person income of $5,963, or $16.34 per person per day. That isn't a lot, but it is much more than the World Bank's "extreme poverty" line of $1.25 per day. This figure is in 2005 U.S. dollars, which is equivalent to $1.53 in 2014 dollars, and it is intended to mark the minimum amount on which one can meet one's basic needs. Globally, more than a billion people are living in extreme poverty, as thus defined, virtually all of them in developing countries. You may be thinking that this figure could be misleading because of the greater purchasing power of money in poorer countries, but that is already taken into account. The World Bank's figure is at "purchasing power parity"—in other words, it is the amount that, in the local currency in the country in which the person lives, buys the same amount of food and other essentials that one can buy for $1.53 in the United States in 2014.[9] If there are any legal residents of the United States living below the World Bank's extreme poverty line, they must be missing out on benefits to which they are entitled because the Supplemental Nutritional Assistance Program, or SNAP (formerly known as food stamps), provides an average monthly benefit of $125 per person, or $4.00 per day.[10] In 2014 nearly forty-seven million relatively poor Americans were participating in SNAP. All impoverished Americans have access to safe drinking water, free schooling for their children, free health care through Medicaid and, in many cases, subsidized public housing. Should they fall seriously ill, they can go to a hospital emergency room, and the hospital will be legally bound to treat them, irrespective of whether they have health insurance, until it is safe for them to be discharged. Hundreds of millions of people in developing countries lack these benefits.

Those who are poor in the United States are poor relative to the majority of members of a society that is, by historical standards, extraordinarily affluent. Those who are in extreme poverty in developing countries, on the other hand, are poor by an absolute standard that refers to their inability to meet their basic needs. In the United States, food security is officially defined as "access by all people at all times to enough food for an active, healthy life."[11] A family is therefore considered to be food insecure if one member does not, for an unspecified period of time, have access to that level of food.[12] This could happen if, for instance, the adults in the family buy diet sodas with their SNAP entitlements (which is perfectly legal) or if they sell their benefits at a discount for cash to buy drugs or alcohol (which is not legal but does happen). In the United States, if child welfare officials discover children who are severely undernourished, they will place the children in care to ensure they are properly fed. In developing countries, poor families may be short of food for long periods, and their children may be permanently stunted because of malnutrition and undernutrition. Poor women often have to walk for three hours a day to fetch water from a stream and then spend more time gathering firewood to boil it to make it safe to drink. If children get diarrhea, their parents are likely to be unable to get any medical assistance for them. Poor parents may have to watch their children die from easily treatable conditions.

I am not denying that Americans should be deeply concerned about poverty in their own country. Other affluent nations have better social security than the United States, so their poor are, in absolute terms, generally better off than the poor in the United States, but in those countries, too, there are grounds for trying to do better. I have no doubt that being poor in a rich nation makes life extremely difficult and often degrading. My point is only that there is a wide gulf between being poor in the United States and being in extreme poverty as defined by the World Bank. For effective altruists, the most important consequence of this gulf is that their dollars go much further when used to aid those outside the affluent nations. We have already seen this in regard to interventions to protect health. The income figures I have noted make it easy to see that this also holds for other benefits, including direct cash transfers. If a family of four is on the extreme poverty line, its annual income will have the purchasing power equivalent of US$2,234. The charity GiveDirectly makes one-off cash grants of about US$1,000 to African families living in extreme poverty. If the families are on or close to the extreme poverty line, this is equivalent to giving them at least six months' income, and if they are well below the extreme poverty line, it may be as much as a year's income. With part of that money, they may buy corrugated iron to replace the leaky thatch on their roof. This keeps the family and its provisions dry when it rains and saves them the cost of replacing the thatch each year. They may use the remainder to start a small business or simply buy more food so the family can eat better. Giving $1,000 to a family living in poverty in the United States might be the equivalent of a month's income. If they are in public housing and using their SNAP benefits well, they will not need the money for food or shelter. If, on the other hand, they are hungry because they are not using their SNAP benefits to buy nourishing food, then we need to know whether they will use $1,000 in cash any better. For all these reasons it is unlikely that $1,000 will bring a poor family in America the kind of benefits that giving the same sum to an impoverished African family will achieve.[13] So whether we prefer to give cash grants or food or health care interventions, we will do more good by donating to organizations working to help people living in extreme poverty in poor nations.

Robert Wiblin has called the difference in what you can get for donations to different charities altruistic arbitrage. In the business world, if two identical products are selling at different prices in different markets and the cost of transporting the products from the lower-priced market to the higher-priced market is less than the price difference, someone will soon buy where the price is lower and sell where the price is higher. That is known as arbitrage, and it tends to smooth out such price differences. If the world of philanthropy were like the business world, then whenever there is an opportunity to do good much more cheaply than most people are doing good, philanthropists would pounce on it, and the opportunity would rapidly disappear. But philanthropy is not as focused on effectiveness as the financial sector is focused on profit. Some causes are less popular than others and so tend to be neglected. That explains why it is possible to do so much more good per dollar donated by helping poor people in poor nations than poor people in rich nations. The rich people in rich nations, either through their government or through domestic charities, are already helping their poorer fellow citizens—perhaps not enough to raise them out of poverty but enough so that the cost of making a lasting, positive difference to the life of a poor American is far higher than the cost of making such a difference to the life of someone who is poor by global standards. Wiblin offers this advice: "Target groups you care about that other people mostly don't, and take advantage of strategies other people are biased against using."[14]

11

Are Some Causes Objectively Better than Others?

Let's return to the Rockefeller Philanthropy Advisors' leaflet "Finding Your Focus in Philanthropy." After setting out the various categories in the manner described in the previous chapter, the leaflet asks, "What is the most urgent issue?" and answers by saying, "There's obviously no objective answer to that question." This is the wrong question to ask, but even if it were the right question, the answer would be wrong.

"What is the most urgent issue?" is not the right question to ask because a potential donor should be asking, "Where can I do the most good?" Consider my own situation, in 1972–73, when I wrote about two separate causes: global poverty, in "Famine, Affluence and Morality," and the treatment of animals, in "Animal Liberation."[1] These were not the only issues around at the time—the Vietnam War was still being fought, and the threat of nuclear war between the United States and the Soviet Union could not be ignored. I was already a vegetarian, had marched against the Vietnam War, and was donating to Oxfam. Where should I direct my time, energy, and whatever ability I might have to argue in favor of one of these causes? I didn't try to answer that question by thinking about which issue is the most *urgent* in the sense of Which issue is most in need of *immediate* action? or even Which issue is it most *important* to resolve?, but by thinking about where I could make the *most difference*. And that, I decided, was the issue of animal suffering because whereas there were many highly able people already campaigning and writing about global poverty, the Vietnam War, and nuclear disarmament, very few thoughtful people were advocating a radical change in the moral status of animals. There was an animal welfare movement, but it was mostly concerned with cruelty to dogs and cats and horses; only a minuscule amount of attention was going to farm animals, where the overwhelming majority of the suffering humans inflict on animals was, and still is, occurring.

For a contemporary example of a similar situation, compare climate change and malaria. On the basis of what the overwhelming majority of scientists in the relevant fields tell us, the need for an international agreement to reduce greenhouse gas emissions is extremely urgent. There are, however, already many governments and organizations working toward getting such an agreement. It is difficult for private donors to be confident that anything they can do will make that agreement more likely. In contrast, distributing mosquito nets to protect children from malaria is, at least from a global perspective, less urgent, but individuals can more easily make a difference to the number of nets distributed. So we should be asking not What is most urgent? but Where can I have the biggest positive impact? That means not just the biggest impact right now or this month or this year, but over the longest period for which it is possible to foresee the consequences of my actions.

If we ask that question, is it still obvious that it has no objective answer?

Suppose you have $100,000 available to donate to the best cause you can find. Your local art museum is seeking funds to build a new wing to have space to display more of its collection. At the same time, you are asked to donate to an organization seeking to carry out surgeries to restore vision among people with trachoma in developing countries. Let's look at what you are choosing between, in terms of the good you could expect your money to achieve. Suppose the new museum wing will cost $50 million, and over the fifty years of its expected useful life one million people will enjoy seeing it each year, for a total of fifty million enhanced museum visits. Since you would contribute 1/500th of the cost, you could claim credit for the enhanced aesthetic experiences of one hundred thousand visitors. What if you donate to cure blindness? If we use the most conservative of the figures discussed in the previous chapter, we can say that it costs, on average, $100 per case of blindness cured or averted, so a donation of $100,000 could be expected to restore or preserve the sight of one thousand poor people in developing countries.

On the one side, then, we have enhanced aesthetic experiences for one hundred thousand museum visitors, and on the other side we have one thousand people spared fifteen years of blindness, with all the problems that that causes for poor people with no social security. A blind person is likely to be unable to work, so the family will lose income or, in the case of a woman with young children to look after, the oldest daughter often has to leave school to assist her and so misses out on the opportunities that education provides. The problem now is to compare these two highly dissimilar outcomes and say which one we should seek to produce.

Intuitively, one might answer the question in this way: The difference between avoiding fifteen years of blindness and not seeing a new wing of an art museum is so great that we don't need to take account of the numbers. There is *no* number of enhanced museum visits that would outweigh restoring sight to someone who will otherwise be blind for so long. The Harvard philosopher Thomas Scanlon defends a view like this when he invites us to imagine a situation in which a technician suffers an accident in the transmitter room of a television station during the broadcast of a football match. The technician is in severe pain, which cannot be stopped without interrupting the broadcast and diminishing the pleasure of all the fans watching. The match still has an hour to run. According to Scanlon, it doesn't matter how many fans are enjoying the game; even if there are a billion of them, we should not attempt to add up their pleasures and see if they outweigh the pain of the technician. When we are faced with the needs of those who are, in Scanlon's words, "severely burdened," the sum of the smaller pleasures of the many have no "justificatory weight."[2]

Intuitively appealing as this answer might be, and notwithstanding the support it gives for directing one's donations to helping the global poor rather than to museums, many effective altruists will be uncomfortable with the idea of setting a cutoff line for severe burdens against which a vast number of lesser harms simply do not matter.[3] For those who share this discomfort there is, fortunately, an alternative way of defending the view that we ought to use our funds to cure one thousand people of fifteen years of blindness rather than to enhance the museum experiences of one hundred thousand visitors.

Try this thought experiment: suppose you have a choice between visiting the art museum, including its new wing, or going to see the museum without visiting the new wing. Naturally, you'd prefer to see it with the new wing. But now imagine that an evil demon doesn't like the new wing, and so from every one hundred people who see it he chooses one at random and inflicts fifteen years of blindness on that person. Would you still visit the new wing? You'd have to be nuts. Even if the evil demon blinded only one person in every one thousand, in my judgment (and I predict in most people's judgment) seeing the museum's new wing still would not be worth the risk. If you agree, then you are saying, in effect, that the harm of one person's becoming blind outweighs the benefits received by one thousand people visiting the new wing. Therefore a donation that saves one person from becoming blind would be better value than a donation that enables one thousand people to visit the new wing. But in deciding where to give your donation, you are choosing between enhancing the museum visits of one hundred thousand people or saving one thousand people from blindness. That's a ratio of 100:1, not 1,000:1. If you agreed that you would not take your chances with the evil demon, even if he blinded only one in every one thousand visitors, then you are, in effect, agreeing that a donation to prevent or cure blindness offers at least ten times the value of giving to the museum. If you would see the new wing if the demon blinded one in every thousand, but not if he blinded one in every two hundred, you are implicitly valuing a donation to prevent or cure blindness at twice the value of giving to the museum.

Similar methods of comparing very different kinds of benefits are used by economists to judge how much people value certain states of affairs. Such methods are open to criticism because many people appear to have irrational attitudes toward small risks of very bad things happening. (That's why we need legislation requiring people in cars to wear seat belts.) An alternative way of thinking about the choice is to ask how many hours or days of blindness you would accept in exchange for seeing the new wing. Fifteen years is 5,475 days, so unless you would be willing to be blind for 54.75 days in order to see the new wing, you are agreeing that donating to prevent or cure trachoma does more good than donating to the museum. If you would be unwilling to be blind even for 5.475 days in order to see the new wing, your choices imply that donating to the trachoma charity offers ten times the value of donating to the museum. (These calculations do not even take into account the fact that knowing you will regain your sight after the specified number of days will make your blindness much easier to bear.)[4]

When we make our choices in the real world, we need to have the best possible information. The figures I gave for the benefits to be gained from building the new museum wing were tweaked to make the arithmetic simple, but they are not unrealistic. In 1987 the Metropolitan Museum of Art in New York built the Lila Acheson Wallace Wing to house its collection of modern art, at a cost of $26 million, equivalent to $54 million in 2014 dollars. In 2014 the Met announced it would rebuild the wing, "possibly from scratch," in which case it will not have lasted even the fifty years I estimated for a new wing in my example. The new wing will probably cost a lot more than $50 million. "Projects of this scale," the *New York Times* commented, "typically cost hundreds of millions of dollars." The museum attracts over six million visitors each year, but few go to every gallery, and as modern art is not the Met's strength, an estimate of one million visitors per year is reasonable. (For comparison, when the museum opened new galleries for American paintings, sculpture, and decorative arts in 2012, it took eighteen months for the galleries to reach a total of one million visitors—approximately 11 percent of the museum's total attendance during that period.) The expansion and renovation of the Museum of Modern Art in New York (MoMA), completed in 2004, cost $858 million, or seventeen times as much as the hypothetical museum in my example; on the other hand, MoMA receives about three million visitors each year, or three times as many as in my example.[5] That yields a cost per visitor more than five times higher than in the example. The remaining uncertainty is the cost of preventing or curing blindness, but the margin of error in my example is great enough for us to conclude that the sums the Metropolitan Museum of Art and MoMA have spent and are planning to spend on their extensions and renovations would have done more good if used to restore or preserve the sight of people too poor to pay for such treatment themselves. I am not suggesting that these museums should have done that. They were set up for a different purpose, and to use their funds to help the global poor would presumably be a breach of their founding deeds or statutory obligations and could invite litigation from past donors who may perceive it as a violation of the purposes for which they had donated. (Perhaps, though, the museums could justify, as part of their mission, restoring sight in people who would then be able to visit and appreciate the art they display?) Individual donors, however, are not bound by any founding deeds or obligations to their past donors. They should be thinking about how their funds can do the most good. We can now see that giving them to art museums for a renovation or expansion would not do the most good.

In response to an earlier critique of mine that appeared in the *New York Times*, Melissa Berman, the president and chief executive of Rockefeller Philanthropy Advisors, defended the approach taken in their leaflet.[6] Her letter touches on the importance of art, on personal convictions about causes to support, and on the question of objectivity. On art, she writes, "The arts are not simply transitory entertainment. They are how we share culture, challenge thinking and experience the world. They are an economic engine and an aid to learning." When Aaron Moore put all his belongings up for sale in an art gallery, he was challenging our thinking on an important issue, and all the money raised went to help the poor, so he did make some difference, but it would be a struggle to name many other contemporary artists of whom one could say the same.[7] Jeff Koons has emphasized the importance of art's social dimension: "If art is not directed toward the social," he has said, "it becomes purely self-indulgent, like sex without love." That raises the obvious question: has Koons's art changed society, and, if so, in what way?

In the interview in which he made the remark just quoted, Koons refers to what he calls "the 'Jim Beam' work" displayed at an exhibition called *Luxury and Degradation*, which, according to the *New York Times*, examined "shallowness, excess and the dangers of luxury in the high-flying 1980s." The work is described as a "stainless-steel train nine and a half feet long filled with bourbon."[8] Koons says it "used the metaphors of luxury to define class structure," adding that it "stands in opposition" to the trend of society dividing into only two groups, people with high income and people with low income.[9] Unfortunately, the fate of Koons's bourbon-filled train bears witness to the capacity of the art world to co-opt works of art, irrespective of their creators' aims, and turn them into items of consumption for the rich. When Christie's auctioned Koons's "Jim Beam" work in 2014, it sold for $33.7 million, a price that suggests it appealed to the very group to which it was conceived as standing in opposition.[10] In fact, it became in reality what it was intended to be a metaphor of: an item of luxury and degradation.

Art surely can be an aid to learning, but building new museums is not likely to be the most cost-effective way to do that. We have other opportunities for studying art from which we will learn as much or more than we can by joining the crowds peering at very expensive paintings from behind a rope or through bulletproof glass. If the goal were really to educate the public about art, museums would do better to spend a few thousand dollars on the highest-quality reproductions and allow the public to get as close to them as they like.

To forestall misunderstandings: there is value in creating and enjoying art. To many people, drawing, painting, sculpting, singing, and playing a musical instrument are vital forms of self-expression, and their lives would be poorer without them. People produce art in all cultures and in all kinds of situations, even when they cannot satisfy their basic physical needs. Other people enjoy seeing art. In a world in which everyone had enough to eat, basic health care, adequate sanitation, and a place at school for each of their children, there would be no problem about donating to museums and other institutions that offer an opportunity to see original works of art to all who wish to see them, and (more important, in my view) the opportunity to create art to those who lack opportunities to express themselves in this way. Sadly, we don't live in that world, at least not yet.

Berman draws on the experience of Rockefeller Philanthropy Advisors to explain why it is best to allow potential donors to follow their "personal convictions" in choosing a charity. Doing so leads, she observes, to their giving more and more consistently. This may be so, but if the price of trying to persuade people to donate to the cause that does the most good is that they give less, that price may be worth paying. To decide if it is, we would have to compare the amount of good a dollar will do if donated to the charity that best accords with the donor's initial personal convictions with the amount of good a dollar will do if donated to the best charity to which we could persuade the donor to donate. As we have seen, some charities do hundreds, even thousands, of times more good per dollar than others. Donating to restore sight rather than to train a guide dog is one example. The World Bank employee I have called Gorby found, even among projects the bank had already vetted and was willing to fund, a sixfold difference in the cost of preventing an unwanted birth.[11] So even if donors give much less when advisors try to persuade them not to follow their initial inclinations about where they should give, the outcome may still be better. A donor might, for example, give half as much, but the charity may do a hundred times as much good per dollar it receives; then persuading the donor to give to the more effective charity will lead to benefits fifty times greater than leaving the donor to follow her or his initial personal convictions.

Moreover, in some cases, leaving people to pursue their personal convictions does harm instead of good. In the United States they might, for example, make a tax-deductible donation to the National Rifle Association's Whittington Center. This charity is described on the association's "Firearms for Freedom" website as "America's finest shooting facility," offering "an abundance of ranges, a shotgun shooting center, guided and unguided hunts, and an adventure camp for younger shooters."[12] If trying to persuade someone not to donate to an NRA-affiliated charity meant that they stopped giving altogether, that would be a positive outcome. Even if the charity does no harm while doing only a modest amount of good, the fact that the donation is tax-deductible means that taxpayers pay for about 40 percent of donations from high-income people. This draws money away from areas of government that do more good than the charity.

In any case, whether it is wise to push people to give to the objectively best cause is a separate issue from whether some causes are objectively better than others. The answer to the former question depends on the consequences of pushing people to give to the objectively best cause. In weighing these consequences, we should take into account that the only strong conviction some donors will have is that they want to do the most good they can with the resources they have available. We should encourage this attitude to giving. Telling people that there is "obviously no objective answer" to such a question can only dampen their enthusiasm for pursuing this laudable quest.

12

Difficult Comparisons

I have argued that there are objective answers to the question, What is the best cause? That doesn't mean it is always possible to determine what that answer is. Starting with my example of treating blindness, Berman invites us to compare a variety of causes: "If $100,000 can prevent blindness in 1,000 people, is that better than using $100,000 to feed the starving? Rescue abused animals? Protect women from rape? Keep glaciers frozen? Provide education? Housing? Accountable government? There are no precise answers to these questions, and sound impact assessment won't create them. It will only allow us to compare programs addressing similar objectives with one another. It won't tell us whose fate is most worth changing. Hard as it is, we must each answer that question for ourselves." In some of these cases, methods of making such comparisons exist, although they raise deep philosophical questions and so remain controversial. For comparing other causes, we really have no such methods.

Let's begin by considering the first comparison Berman raises, between spending $100,000 on preventing blindness or on feeding the starving. Berman allows us to suppose that we know that for $100,000 we can cure blindness in one thousand people, but we also need to know how many lives we will save by spending $100,000 on feeding the starving. That will depend on the specific circumstances in which people are starving, so let's just imagine that with $100,000 we can save the lives of five hundred starving people, who will then have a normal life expectancy for their region.

Now we need to compare curing blindness with saving lives. At first glance, that might seem impossible, but the field of health economics has a substantial literature on making such comparisons, and several countries use methods developed by health economists to decide how to allocate their health care resources. In the United Kingdom, for instance, the National Institute for Health and Care Excellence, known as NICE, uses such methods in order to recommend to the National Health Service authorities which drugs and treatments they should provide free of charge to British residents who can benefit from them. In contrast to the United States, where politicians cannot bring themselves to say the word *rationing* in the context of health care, the British government is open about the fact that some treatments, though beneficial, are poor value and should not be provided. To reach this conclusion, NICE, for each treatment it considers, draws on estimates of the cost of gaining a quality-adjusted life-year, or QALY. To understand this idea, imagine yourself with some serious, permanent health condition, perhaps one that confines you to bed. Suppose your life expectancy is forty years. Now a physician offers you a new treatment that will restore you to normal health. But there is a catch: the new treatment will reduce your life expectancy. Naturally, the first question you ask the physician is, "Reduce it by *how much?*" But the physician has to take an urgent call before she can answer your question, leaving you to ponder how great a reduction in life expectancy you will accept in order to regain normal health. Will the new treatment cut ten years off your life? To get out of bed and live normally again for thirty years would be worth that, so you'd take it. Will it shorten your life by thirty years? No thanks! After going back and forth between the cases where you are reasonably clear about your answers, you finally reach the point of equilibrium, at which you can't really decide whether or not to have the treatment. Suppose that point is twenty years, so that to regain normal health you have to give up half of your life expectancy. We can then say that, for you, a year of life confined to bed is worth only 0.5 of a year of life in normal health. If your point of indifference were a reduced life expectancy of ten years, you would be valuing a year of life in your condition at 0.75 of a year of normal life, and if the point of indifference were a thirty-year reduction, you would be saying that a year of your present life is worth only 0.25 of a year in normal health. Whatever your decision, you would have arrived at a way of trading off the loss to you that is caused by your condition, against the loss to you that would be caused by your death. This makes it possible for us to do cost-effectiveness estimates that compare curing your condition with saving your life.

The World Health Organization (WHO) has developed a similar concept to deal with a comparable kind of problem. In order to set priorities, WHO wanted to estimate the global burden of various diseases. To do that it had to make just the comparisons that Berman mentions—for example, to compare the burden of diseases that cause people to become blind with diseases that cause people to die. For this purpose WHO uses the Disability-Adjusted Life-Year, or DALY. One DALY represents one year of life in full health. As with QALYs, a year of life with a disability is discounted according to the severity of the disability. The extent of the discounting is decided by various methods involving interviews with samples of the population. For the WHO study of the Global Burden of Disease for 2010, a large team of researchers carried out nearly fourteen thousand face-to-face interviews in several countries and supplemented these findings with a web survey. The researchers found generally consistent results across distinct cultures. For blindness, it indicated a discount of 0.2.[1] In other words, 1 year when blind is equivalent to 0.8 years of healthy life, or curing a person of blindness for 5 years is equivalent to extending a healthy person's life by 1 year. At that discount rate, using the hypothetical figures mentioned above, in the populations we could help for $100,000, untreated blindness causes the loss of 1,000 x 0.2 = 200 DALYs per year, while starvation threatens to cause the loss of 500 DALYs per year. On these figures, we should feed the starving.

It is not difficult to find grounds for disagreeing with this discount rate for blindness and with the methods used to evaluate various health states.[2] Whom should we ask to do this evaluation: ordinary members of the public? or those with the condition? On the one hand, there is plenty of psychological research casting doubt on the reliability of judgments by people in good health about what it would be like to suffer from adverse health conditions. On the other hand, people who have adjusted to such a condition may have forgotten how much better it was to be in good health. Even people who have recently had a painful experience and are asked how bad it was seem to be subject to illusions.[3]

GiveWell has raised other questions about DALYs. In a blog post Holden Karnofsky asks us to imagine that, for the same cost, we could accomplish any of the following:

1. Prevent 100 deaths-in-infancy, knowing that in all likelihood these 100 people will grow up to have consistently low income and poor health for their ~40-year-long lives.

2. Provide consistent, full nutrition and health care to 100 people, such that instead of growing up malnourished (leading to lower height, lower weight, lower intelligence,

and other symptoms) they spend their lives relatively healthy. (For simplicity, though not accuracy, assume this doesn't affect their actual lifespan—they still live about 40 years.)

3. Prevent one case of relatively mild non-fatal malaria (say, a fever that lasts a few days) for each of 10,000 people, without having a significant impact on the rest of their lives.[4]

Holden reports that he would choose (2) because he is "very excited by the idea of changing someone's life in a lasting and significant way." He rejects (3) because he doesn't think the quality of a life consists simply in the sum of the quality of the days in it, and he rejects (1) because he doesn't put much value on "potential lives," especially when the lives lived, if the potential is realized, will be riddled with health problems.

In a subsequent blog post Holden noted that some comments on his previous post agreed with his view and others didn't, adding, "It's possible that we would all agree if we knew more about the lives of people in the developing world, or if we just had long enough to argue about our values. It's also possible that we wouldn't." The relevance of this to GiveWell's work is that any disagreement on these fundamental value questions will lead to disagreement about the cost-effectiveness of different health care interventions, and converting the benefits of those interventions into a single figure like the DALY obfuscates the disagreement rather than resolving it.[5] Holden is in a situation like that of Berman insofar as they are both involved in advising donors. The advice that should be given, he thinks, is that for $100,000, for example, you can restore health to X people or save the lives of Y infants. Then donors can decide in accordance with their values. To that extent, Holden agrees with Berman that with some choices there is no objective method of deciding which option is better.

Toby Ord, commenting on Holden's blog post, agrees that there are serious problems with the DALY approach but supports it as the "best attempt so far" to produce a single metric that will allow people to decide between different health care interventions. "If there really are strongly convincing arguments that it should be tweaked in way X or Y," he adds, "then presumably it will be and will continue to evolve."[6] Toby is right to say we should continue to work to construct a single measure of well-being, even if we know we will not reach it in the near- to medium-term future. In the absence of such a metric, governments and international bodies like the WHO that allocate limited resources to health care are prone to be swayed by those with the loudest voices and best lobbyists. A substantial amount of research has gone into developing ways of measuring the benefits of health care interventions, and we should not abandon the attempt. I am hopeful that if we could reach agreement about all the relevant facts, we might then, given enough time and goodwill, end up agreeing about our values. In the absence of the necessary conditions for reaching such agreement, however, GiveWell's strategy for advising potential donors makes sense. The fact that we should adopt that strategy in regard to the value disparities to which it points, however, does not show that the same is true of other questions, such as supporting art museums rather than restoring sight. Presumably GiveWell agrees with this, as it does not evaluate charities that support museums. In its initial years it did consider some charities that assist the poor in the United States, but it soon ceased to do so because it judged that there is more value to be gained per dollar spent on helping the global poor. Presumably GiveWell thinks there are some value questions on which people can reasonably differ and others on which they cannot.

Another item on Berman's list of causes among which she thinks there is no objective way of choosing is "Protect women from rape." Everyone who is not a rapist would, presumably, like to protect women from rape, but one can't even discuss whether charities that have this goal are worth supporting until one has some idea of how they will go about achieving it. Suppose we continue with the hypothetical scenario that we can cure a case of blindness for $100 or save the life of someone who is starving for $200. How much shall we say that it costs to prevent, on average, one rape per year? If it would cost $1 million, we would then have to face the conclusion that preventing rape should not be our top priority. Failing to prevent a single rape, bad as it is, is surely not as bad as failing to save five thousand lives. The only way one might think that it is would be to hold that the greatest evil is to be found not in the harm suffered by the victim but in the evil intentions of the perpetrator. Some Roman Catholics may hold this view. In a famous passage, Cardinal John Henry Newman wrote, "[The Church] holds that it were better for sun and moon to drop from heaven, for the earth to fail, and for all the many millions who are upon it to die of starvation in extremest agony, so far as temporal affliction goes, than that one soul, I will not say, should be lost, but should commit one single venial sin, should tell one wilful untruth, though it harmed no one, or steal one poor farthing without excuse."[7] For Newman, this evaluation followed from the belief, which he shared, that this world is "dust and ashes, compared with the value of one single soul." To nonbelievers, Newman's position is appalling. Effective altruists will reject it emphatically. Newman was beatified as recently as 2010, however, which suggests that his view may still have some support within Roman Catholic circles.

Berman also mentions donating for education and housing, though without saying whether she has in mind domestic education and housing or education and housing in developing countries. For reasons already explained, if we are donating for education or housing we are likely to get much greater value per dollar if we provide these benefits for people in extreme poverty in poor countries than if we do it in rich countries. If, however, we are comparing charities that provide education and housing for people in extreme poverty, it is not, in principle, impossible to compare the benefits achieved by such charities with benefits achieved by restoring sight or preventing starvation. Admittedly, in practice such comparisons are difficult because the benefits of education may take years to become manifest. Nevertheless, all of these charities really have a common goal: trying to improve the well-being of the poor. That means that if we could know all the relevant facts, we would have an objective basis for judging one type of charity to be likely to do more than another, for the same cost, toward achieving that goal.

13

Reducing Animal Suffering and
Protecting Nature

Berman includes "rescue abused animals" as another of the charitable causes which she appears to believe cannot be objectively compared with other causes. Presumably she has in mind charities that
rescue pets, mostly dogs and cats, and attempt to find homes for
them, for that is the focus of most animal rescue organizations.[1]
There is, however, a straightforward reason for not giving the highest
priority to charities that rescue abused animals. The suffering of
abused pets amounts to a tiny fraction of the suffering we inflict on
animals. In 2012 there were 164 million owned dogs and cats in the
United States.[2] The majority of them probably live reasonably good
lives, but even if every single one of them were abused, this number
would be dwarfed by the 9.1 billion animals annually raised and
slaughtered for food in the United States.[3] Factory-farmed animals
have to endure a lifetime of suffering much more severe than the
typical dog or cat, and in the United States there are fifty-five times
as many factory-farmed animals as there are dogs and cats. Anyone
who kept a dog confined in the way that breeding sows are frequently
confined in factory farms—in crates so small they cannot even turn
around or walk a single step—would be liable to prosecution for
cruelty.

In *The Animal Activists' Handbook* Matt Ball and Bruce Friedrich make a startling claim that vividly illustrates the vastly greater suffering of animals raised for food compared to other ways in which we cause animals to suffer: "Every year, hundreds of millions of animals—*many times more* than the total number killed for fur, housed in shelters, and locked in laboratories combined—don't even make it to slaughter. They actually *suffer to death.*"[4]

Think about what Ball and Friedrich are saying. They are not describing the number of animals killed for food. They are talking about animals who don't even get the "benefit" of supposedly humane slaughter laws because they are so badly treated that they die before they ever get to slaughter. The numbers include caged hens pecked to death because they are unable to get away from their stressed, aggressive fellow prisoners; broiler chickens bred to grow so fast that their immature legs collapse under them, and they then die of thirst or hunger in the broiler shed because they cannot reach the feeders; and pigs, cattle, turkeys, and chickens who were alive when packed into transports but die from the stress that transport imposes on animals who have lived their entire lives indoors. Harish Sethu has done the sums for the United States on his website Counting Animals. The total number of animals killed in shelters each year is around 4 million, for fur 10 million, and in laboratories 11.5 million, making a total of approximately 25.5 million. Using conservative figures based on industry reports and scientific journals, Sethu estimates that 139 million chickens suffer to death annually. Adding turkeys, pigs, and cattle would increase this figure.[5]

Despite this immense disproportion, because our pets are so much more popular than chickens or pigs or cows, there are thousands of organizations in the United States working to help dogs and cats and relatively few working for farmed animals. Animal Charity

Evaluators (ACE) acknowledges that by sterilizing dogs and cats, curtailing the spread of disease among them, and finding good homes for some animals in shelters it is possible to reduce the suffering and killing of dogs and cats; but this comes at a high cost because it includes medical care, vaccines, and the provision of food and housing. Hence, ACE says, "it seems unlikely that this is a cost-effective method to alleviate suffering." Instead, ACE concludes that the most effective way to help animals and prevent the largest amount of suffering is to be an advocate for farm animals. Whereas animal rescue will cost tens or even hundreds of dollars per animal saved, convincing people to reduce or eliminate their consumption of animal products saves animals at a fraction of this cost. At the time of writing, ACE's recommended charities are both focused on farm animals.[6] This is an instance of the altruistic arbitrage discussed at the conclusion of chapter 9: we should follow Robert Wiblin's advice to focus on the causes that most people don't care about. This is where altruists will find the low-hanging fruit.

The inclusion of animals on Berman's list of causes does, admittedly, raise a more difficult question: How can we compare the good achieved by helping animals with the good achieved by other charities? Here, two separate questions are often confused. One is a factual question: Do animals suffer as much as humans? The other is ethical: Given that an animal is suffering as much as a human, does the suffering of the animal matter as much as the suffering of the human?

The answer to the ethical question should be yes. In *Animal Liberation* I argue that to give less consideration to the interests of non-human animals, merely because they are not members of our species, is speciesism and is wrong in much the same way that the crudest forms of racism and sexism are wrong. Speciesism is a form of discrimination against the interests of those who are not "us," where the line between us and the outsiders is drawn on the basis of something that is not in itself morally relevant. My impression is that the moral irrelevance of species, in itself, has come to be accepted by most philosophers who reflect on the question.[7]

The rejection of speciesism is not, however, the end of the debate about the moral weight we should give to animal suffering. Defenders of the way we treat animals usually point out that humans are more rational or autonomous or self-aware or capable of reciprocating than nonhuman animals.[8] To argue on these grounds is to defend not speciesism but the distinct view that we should give more weight to the interests of beings who are rational or autonomous or self-aware or capable of reciprocating. This argument falls short of defending the way we currently treat humans and nonhumans, however, because there are some humans who manifestly have these characteristics to a lesser degree than some nonhumans. Compare, for instance, dogs with human infants less than a month old or chimpanzees with some profoundly intellectually disabled humans. To put aside the possible complications of the potential of a normal infant, we can think only about profoundly intellectually disabled humans. If a nonhuman animal is on the same mental level as a human being—or is superior to the human—and the human has no potential to surpass the level of the animal, then arguments based on the special value of beings with higher cognitive capacities will not justify giving more weight to the human, and we wrong animals whenever we give less weight to their interests than we would, in the same circumstances, give to a human with similar capacities.

Some find it offensive to compare the suffering of humans with that of animals. Presumably they believe that human suffering is always incomparably more important than the suffering of animals. If that is not to be simply a statement of bias toward our own species, it must be based on differences between the mental lives of humans and those of animals. That would mean that we also can't compare the suffering of normal humans with that of humans at a similar mental level to that of nonhuman animals. In any case, even if we focus only on the treatment of animals, the implications of denying the possibility of comparing the suffering of animals with that of humans are sufficient to show that we do make such comparisons. If human suffering were incomparably more important than animal suffering, then any amount of human suffering, no matter how minor, would justify ignoring any amount of animal suffering, no matter how major. If a flock of chickens is without water on a hot day, and all you have to do to prevent them from dying slowly and painfully is turn on a tap, you ought to turn it on. If to do so you have to walk a few extra steps in shoes that pinch your little toe, you ought to walk those few extra steps. Once we acknowledge that some amount of chicken suffering can outweigh some human suffering, however, it doesn't seem so absurd to start reducing the numbers of chickens affected and increasing the amount of human suffering, until we get closer to an equilibrium between the two, or if not that, at least to an area of uncertainty in which neither the chicken suffering nor the human suffering clearly outweighs the other.[9]

To say that we are justified in comparing the sufferings of humans with those of nonhuman animals and that we wrong animals if we give less weight to their sufferings than we give to the similar sufferings of humans is not to deny that there are capacities possessed by normal humans beyond infancy that make a difference to how we should assess interests. Among those capacities might be, for example, the capacity to understand that one exists over time and to form desires about one's future because arguably this gives one a distinct kind of interest in continuing to live that the many nonhuman animals who lack the capacity to form such desires do not have.[10] We can also acknowledge that different levels of awareness may make a difference to how much beings are likely to suffer or enjoy their lives in varying circumstances. This makes it more difficult to compare the good done by reducing the suffering of animals with the good done by, for example, preventing blindness in people with trachoma. Differences in the mental capacities of pigs and chickens also make it difficult to compare the reduction in suffering gained by, say, reforms that prohibit the keeping of hens in cages too small for them to fully stretch their wings with reforms that prohibit keeping sows in crates too narrow for them to turn around. Have we perhaps now reached the point at which there are no sound criteria for choosing one cause rather than another?

We saw in chapter 4 that some effective altruists think that giving to reduce animal suffering is the most effective form of altruism. They are aware of the difficulties just mentioned, but they believe that even if we think farmed animals like chickens, pigs, and cows have less capacity to suffer than human beings, the huge numbers involved and the relatively low cost of making a difference to these numbers by encouraging people to cut down or eliminate the consumption of animal products makes this the most cost-effective way of reducing suffering. Vegan Outreach has, for many years, used volunteers to hand out leaflets at colleges and universities in the United States and is now expanding these activities to other countries. Organizations like The Humane League now use Vegan Outreach leaflets and also do online advertising to lead people to watch videos. The outcomes have been evaluated through follow-ups that seek to estimate the number of people who change their diet as a result of the advertising. ACE has made a careful attempt to establish the cost of averting a year of animal suffering by these techniques. Their research makes estimates of the following:

- Cost per leaflet handed out or, in the case of online ads, cost per click;
- The percentage of those who reduce their consumption of animal products as a result of receiving a leaflet or clicking on an ad;
- The average number of years for which the reduction remains in effect;
- The average number of factory-farmed animals, or their equivalents as dairy and eggs, consumed per person per year;
- The average length of life of the farmed animal (broiler chickens, for example, are killed at forty-two days, so nine factory-farmed chicken lives are equivalent to one year of suffering);
- Elasticity of demand for animal products (to take account of higher consumption by meat-eaters if prices fall as a result of others reducing their consumption).

On this basis, ACE estimates that when leaflets are used, the cost per year of suffering averted is $0.63; with online ads, it is $0.47. ACE acknowledges that the evidence for some of these figures is not robust and is seeking to carry out better studies. In the meantime, it publishes what it believes to be lower and upper bounds on the estimates. For leafleting, ACE's worst-case scenario yields a cost of $12.52 per year of suffering averted; and for online ads, it is $4.52. The best-case scenario for both is less than $0.06.[11] Even if we assume that the worst-case scenario is accurate, these are very inexpensive ways to reduce suffering.

Do animals suffer as intensely as humans? It is hard to know, but on the estimate that ACE believes to be most credible, we could build in assumptions that farmed animals are, for example, capable of only one-tenth as much suffering as humans, and leafleting and online ads about factory farming would still have excellent value compared to the most effective charities helping humans. In addition, when we reduce animal suffering by reducing the consumption of animal products, we get a huge free bonus. Ben West, one of the effective altruists mentioned in chapter 4, has shown that even if your goal were solely to slow down climate change by reducing greenhouse gas emissions, you could do that more effectively by donating to organizations that are encouraging people to go vegetarian or vegan than by donating to leading carbon-offsetting organizations.[12]

Climate Change

I have left until last the cause on Berman's list that she states simply as "Keep glaciers frozen." This could be a reference to the preservation of nature for its own sake or it could stand as a symbol for slowing, stopping, or reversing climate change because there is no way of keeping glaciers frozen without doing that. I'll consider the second possibility first and then return to ask how we should value the preservation of nature for its own sake.

If the Himalayan glaciers disappear, hundreds of millions of people dependent on glacier-fed rivers will be deprived of the water they use to grow their crops. Climate change will also affect rainfall patterns, causing droughts and more severe flooding, and the melting of the Greenland and Antarctic ice sheets will result in a rise in sea levels that will inundate low-lying coastal areas, forcing people who now live there to become refugees. There is some possibility that climate change could spiral out of control in a way that makes our planet uninhabitable, and if that happens before we develop the ability to colonize other planets, it could mean the extinction of our species. That raises a separate ethical question, to which I will return in chapter 15. For the moment, I will assume that climate change will have disastrous effects on many millions and perhaps billions of people but that our species will survive.

It is almost certainly too late to stop or reverse climate change, at least without the use of risky geoengineering techniques.[13] On the other hand, slowing climate change would be a very important goal, one that would bring huge benefits to the global poor and to all future generations. Whether we should support charities seeking to do that will depend on our estimate of the probability that our contribution will affect the ultimate outcome. Because the outcome is so critical, an action that has only a tiny chance of changing that outcome can still have very high expected value. So if one can reasonably believe that this tiny chance exists, then this does seem to be a worthwhile cause. People interested in high-risk, high-payoff causes could rationally donate to it. People who seek a high degree of confidence that their donation will do some measurable good will not. The uncertainties are too great to say whether contributing to an organization that seeks to slow climate change is a better or worse use of $100,000 than restoring sight to one thousand people. That doesn't mean there is no objective answer; it means that we don't have any way of knowing what the objective answer is because we do not have and cannot now get all the relevant facts.

Does Nature Have Intrinsic Value?

Now I can turn to the question of preserving nature for its own sake. *Nature* here may include glaciers, old-growth forests, wild rivers, and endangered species. The choice of preserving or destroying nature will always have some consequences for other sentient beings, whether humans or nonhuman animals. Extinction is, as the slogan says, forever, and once an old-growth forest has been logged it can never be replaced, for any regrowth forest will have characteristics that old-growth forests do not, and the link with something relatively unchanged by human activity will be lost. Hence destroying nature can have negative consequences for an indefinite number of future generations. These considerations provide powerful reasons for protecting nature, even at considerable economic cost. They do not, however, locate this value in nature itself but in the value it has for sentient beings, human and nonhuman, present and future. We therefore should also ask a separate question: Is there value in nature beyond the experiences of sentient beings? Many defenders of wilderness and endangered species argue that there is. When they advocate action to preserve forest or protect endangered species— sometimes killing, in painful ways, large numbers of feral animals in order to do so—they often support their proposals by asserting that biodiversity is an intrinsic value that does not need further justification from arguments that link it to benefits for humans or other sentient beings. The view that nature is intrinsically valuable was memorably expressed by the early American environmentalist Aldo Leopold. In an oft-quoted passage he advocates a "land ethic" according to which an action is right "when it tends to preserve the integrity, stability, and beauty of the biotic community" and wrong when it has the opposite tendency.[14]

Effective altruists have not shown much interest in the intrinsic value of nature. Just as they tend to view values like justice, freedom, equality, and knowledge not as good in themselves but good because of the positive effect they have on social welfare, so they do not value nature as good in itself but instead ask whether preserving nature will be good or bad for animals and humans. Some effective altruists even see nature negatively because of the immense amount of suffering wild animals experience and look forward to a future in which it may be possible to do something to reduce that suffering.[15]

For those who assert that nature has intrinsic value, the comparison of that value with other values, such as the well-being of humans and animals, becomes an insoluble difficulty. My own view, which I have defended elsewhere, is that intrinsic value is to be found only in conscious experiences (not in all conscious experiences but only in positive ones). On this view, nature itself, independently of the sentient beings whose lives it makes possible, does not have intrinsic value, and so the difficulty of comparing its intrinsic value with the intrinsic value of the experiences of sentient beings does not arise.[16]

14

Choosing the Best Organization

Depending on the cause we decide to support, there may be dozens, hundreds, or even thousands of organizations working for it. One key factor that has made effective altruism a practical possibility is the development of metacharities, organizations that evaluate other charities. I've mentioned two of these already: GiveWell and Animal Charity Evaluators. What they are attempting to do is critical to the success of effective altruism, but the field is still at an early stage, and some aspects of it are controversial.

Most gifts to charities are emotionally based. Two-thirds of donors do no research at all before giving.[1] Some give on the basis of photos of children, either happy or emaciated, or of animals, especially those with big round eyes. Others give because they are asked by someone they know—and they do not stop to ask what evidence that person has about the effectiveness of the charity. As we have seen, small donors actually give *less* when they are shown solid evidence that a charity is effective than when they are given no evidence at all.[2] On the other hand, the proportion of donors who do research varies with the area in which they give, and it is not surprising that more donors to international aid organizations do some research (62 percent) than donors to any other cause; at the other end of the spectrum, the figure for donors to the arts who do research is 25 percent and for donors to religion, 22 percent.[3]

Donors do have an excuse for doing no research: it isn't easy to find out how effective a charity is. Before GiveWell began its work, the main way in which donors could check up on a charity was to go to the website of Charity Navigator, which describes itself as "America's largest and most influential charity evaluator." In 2012 Charity Navigator's website had 6.2 million visits. It rates about seven thousand charities, including all of the better-known ones, and has the capacity to rate one hundred new charities a month, but it can do this only because its ratings are so superficial. Until 2011 they were based solely on the financial health of the charity, using information taken from a form that all charities in the United States must provide to the Internal Revenue Service. That form is also one element of a second dimension added after 2011, accountability and transparency. The other element of the assessment of accountability and transparency is the organization's website. None of this information tells us anything about the outcomes of the charity's programs. Charity Navigator plans to add a third dimension that will report on the charities' achievements, but to do that properly for seven thousand charities would be a mammoth undertaking, and Charity Navigator has not set a timetable for doing it.[4]

Many people go to Charity Navigator's website to look at a single figure: the percentage of a charity's revenue that it spends on administration and fund-raising, rather than on its programs. Holden Karnofsky has said that it is scary to think how commonly people use this figure when deciding whether to donate to a charity—and remember, these people are among the minority who do some research before donating.[5] In extreme cases, these figures are meaningful. The Children's Charity Fund, Inc., a small Florida-based organization, spends 84 percent of its revenue on fund-raising activities and nearly 10 percent on administrative expenses, leaving just 6.1 percent for its programs.[6] It gets the lowest possible rating from Charity Navigator.

To warn unwary donors away from such organizations is a useful service. Beyond a few of these cases, however, the proportion of revenue spent on administration and fund-raising doesn't tell us anything about the effectiveness of a charity. An organization may spend very little on administration and fund-raising, but a donation to it may be just as much a waste of money as a donation to the Children's Charity Fund, Inc. You might, for example, face this choice between two charities that aim to help the poor in a developing country:

- Charity A: 8 percent of revenue goes to administration and fund-raising, 92 percent goes to programs
- Charity B: 28 percent of revenue goes to administration and fund-raising, 72 percent goes to programs.

Should you donate to A rather than to B? Unless you know that A's programs are as effective or almost as effective as B's, you don't have enough information to answer that question. Perhaps the reason Charity A spends so much less on administration is that it spends nothing on oversight and evaluation. As a result, the directors of A never discover that its programs are poorly suited to the regions in which they are carried out, and only 10 percent of them benefit the poor. Charity B gets detailed evaluations from its well-qualified staff and by ceasing to fund programs that are not working is able to ensure that 90 percent of its programs help the poor. If you knew this, you could calculate that when you give to A, 8 percent of your donation goes to administration and fund-raising, 83 percent achieves nothing, and 9 percent directly helps the poor, whereas if you give to B, 28 percent of your donation goes to administration and fund-raising, 7.2 percent achieves nothing, and 64.8 percent directly helps the poor. B is the better choice.

GiveWell is at the opposite end of the spectrum to Charity Navigator. Instead of trying to evaluate all kinds of charities, it began with a focus on charities that help the poor. After initially reviewing promising charities working in the United States as well as in developing countries, GiveWell decided, largely for the reasons discussed in chapter 10, that interventions aimed at assisting poor people in developing countries were likely to be much more cost-effective than interventions aimed at assisting the poor in more affluent countries. It therefore ceased to review charities that were not seeking to help the global poor. It has now reviewed hundreds of charities that do aim to help the poor in developing countries, and the more promising of these are reviewed in considerable depth. Only a handful are recommended. That doesn't mean GiveWell has concluded that the other charities are *not* cost-effective; instead it has concluded only that it cannot find sufficient evidence demonstrating that the charities *are* doing good in a cost-effective way. In the absence of such evidence, GiveWell writes a report on the charities it has reviewed, but it does not recommend them.

More recently, GiveWell's high standards have led it to focus not on individual organizations but on specific types of intervention. The reason for this switch is that GiveWell is dissatisfied with evidence that comes from self-evaluations by charities. Evidence of the highest quality, GiveWell contends, is found only in academic research which focuses on the type of intervention (for example, distributing insecticide-treated nets to reduce the burden of malaria; deworming children; providing cash grants to poor families) and not on the charity that is carrying out the intervention. Thus one could describe GiveWell's current mode of investigation as first identifying interventions for which there is rigorous evidence that they have positive effects, and then investigating organizations that focus narrowly on these demonstrably beneficial interventions. GiveWell is also more likely to recommend organizations that encourage independent, high-quality studies of their interventions and are transparent about and ready to learn from the outcomes of these studies.

GiveWell is not able to investigate organizations that do many different things for which there is less evidence of efficacy, even if there are, among these varied activities, some demonstrably beneficial interventions. That is why none of the major aid organizations (Oxfam, CARE, International Red Cross, Doctors Without Borders, UNICEF, Save the Children, World Vision) make it onto the GiveWell list of recommended organizations. It is difficult, GiveWell contends, to evaluate the good done by a dollar given to an organization that will divide it up among many activities, only some of which can be shown to benefit the people they are aiming to assist. Some of these organizations allow donors to direct their donation to one among a range of specific projects, but GiveWell is skeptical that this really makes a difference. The organization will also receive unrestricted gifts and presumably has its own priorities among the projects. If individual donors converge on one or two projects and leave others underfunded, the organization might use some of its unrestricted funds to top-up the underfunded ones. Directing a donation to a specific project thus won't necessarily affect whether or not the project will go ahead or even its scale.

In 2013 GiveWell recommended only three charities, two of which specialize in treating parasitic worm infections that cause children to develop anemia and slow their progress in school, while the third is GiveDirectly, which, as we saw in chapter 5, was founded to give cash grants directly to very poor people. These interventions have been evaluated by randomized controlled trials, the same means that pharmaceutical companies use to test new drugs. Before the intervention, a pool of potential recipients is identified and baseline measurements of their health or well-being are taken. Usually the recipients will be individuals, but in some cases they will be entire villages. Half of them are then selected, at random, to receive the intervention, while the other half do not. At the end of the trial, further measurements are taken from both groups. The randomization makes it possible to isolate the impact of the intervention from other changes that may be occurring in the region at the same time.[7]

Randomized controlled trials are accepted as the ultimate standard of proof in health care. They have frequently shown widely used drugs and medical treatments to be ineffective or less effective than available alternatives, and they can do the same when used for testing aid projects. For example, in many developing countries, children, and in particular girls, do not spend enough time at school, even when school is free, to learn as they should. To change this, the following strategies have been suggested:

- Unconditional cash transfers for girls;
- Cash transfers for girls, conditional on attendance;
- Merit scholarships for girls;
- Free primary school uniforms;
- Deworming through primary schools;
- Providing information to parents about the increased wages of those who stay at school.

All of these strategies look plausible. When resources for education are scarce, as they always are, especially in developing countries, which one should be tried? In the absence of randomized testing, it would be impossible to know. But the Jameel Poverty Action Lab has tested them and found that the last one on the list is by far the most cost-effective. Every $100 spent on providing information to parents about the increased wages of those who stay at school results in an amazing 20.7 additional years spent at school! Deworming through primary schools is also highly cost-effective, leading to 13.9 additional years spent at school per $100 spent. Of the remaining interventions, the first two are relatively ineffective, both gaining less than 1 additional year per $100, and the cash transfers, whether conditional or unconditional, gain less than one-tenth of an additional year per $100.[8] The most effective method thus results in more than two hundred times the benefits of the two least effective methods, which means that for every $100 spent on one of the least effective methods, $99.50 is wasted. When resources are limited and education is so important to the future of children, that waste means that many human beings do not achieve their full potential.

In 2013 Jacob Goldstein and Dave Kestenbaum of the radio program *Planet Money* went to Kenya to compare the work of Give-Directly and Heifer International, which gives cows to poor people. GiveDirectly had arranged for independent researchers to do a randomized controlled trial on the impact of the cash transfers they were giving. Paul Niehaus suggested to Goldstein and Kestenbaum that the way to resolve the question of whether giving cash is better or worse than giving cows is to run a similar trial comparing the two interventions. Goldstein and Kestenbaum put the idea to Elizabeth Bintliff, vice president of Heifer International's Africa programs. Bintliff's reply was, "We're not about experiments. These are lives of real people and we have to do what we believe is correct. We can't make experiments with people's lives. They're just . . . they're people. It's too important."[9]

Bintliff is not the first to claim that it is unethical to do randomized trials. The usual basis of the ethical objection to randomized trials is that to obtain the necessary control group, one must deny the intervention to half of the population that could benefit from it. This objection would gain more traction if we had good grounds for believing that the intervention is beneficial *and* have the option of providing it to everyone who could benefit from it. Presumably, though, limited resources make that impossible for Heifer International. If some people will, in any case, not receive the intervention, it is difficult to see any ethical objection to making use of that fact to learn how beneficial the intervention really is. Anyway, what Niehaus was proposing was not a comparison of giving poor people a cow or doing nothing for them, but of giving cows or cash grants. Heifer International could not know that spending a given sum on providing cows to people leads to better outcomes than providing cash grants.

Randomized controlled trials of drugs and medical treatments are also "experiments with people's lives," but when the trials comply with guidelines set by international research organizations they are widely considered not only permissible, but obligatory. In the long run, they save lives. To those who say it is unethical to "experiment with people's lives," the proper response is that the alternative—failing to use the resources available to improve the lives of as many people as possible—is much worse. Heifer International's unwillingness to put what it is doing to the test suggests that it fears the outcome might not support the specific intervention that is its trademark.

Nevertheless, randomized controlled trials do have drawbacks and limitations. For some aid interventions, getting trained people to remote villages is the largest part of the budget. If randomization is to be done on a village level—which will be necessary in some situations—and one arm of the trial is no intervention, then twice as many villages need to be visited to get the baseline measurements, and so doing a trial can come close to doubling the cost of the project.

Oxfam America wanted to do a randomized trial of its "Savings for Change" program, which encouraged women in rural villages in Mali to set up savings schemes from which each member could borrow money when needed. The trial required investigating six thousand households in five hundred villages. Oxfam staff worried that donors would be concerned to find that almost half of their donation was going to research rather than to directly helping people. The dilemma was resolved when funding for the trial was made available by Innovations for Poverty Action, a research group that gets funding from far-sighted foundations, government bodies, corporations, and individuals in order to assess which antipoverty programs work and which do not. (The study found notable benefits in some areas, including food security, but not in health, school enrollment, investment in small business, or, surprisingly, empowerment of women. It may take more time for such differences to become manifest. On the other hand, it is also possible that the intervention will have less impact than the originators of the project hoped.)[10]

The major limitation of randomized controlled trials is that they can be used only for certain kinds of interventions, in particular, those that can be done on a small scale with hundreds or thousands of individuals or villages, from which samples large enough to yield statistically significant results can be drawn. They are therefore not suited to evaluating country-scale interventions and national or international advocacy programs. Oxfam puts resources into both direct aid and advocacy work. It believes that its advocacy work is better grounded because of the direct aid it does, and at the same time it regards it as vital to try to combat, as far as possible, the causes of poverty. Advocacy for policy change has obvious appeal to those who are concerned that more traditional forms of aid are putting a Band-Aid on the symptoms of poverty rather than dealing with its deeper roots.

Sometimes it is possible to estimate the costs and benefits of advocacy work in ways that make it reasonably clear it is good value. Oxfam has long taken an interest in extractive industries like oil and mining, which often deprive the poor of land or pollute the rivers on which local people rely for fishing, irrigation, and drinking water. Some extractive industries provide employment and revenue for the local economy, but others do not. Hence when, in 2007, commercial quantities of oil and gas were discovered in Ghana, Oxfam took an interest in what would happen to the revenue. Although Ghana is widely regarded as a well-governed democracy, it was by no means certain that this new source of income would benefit the poor, who constitute roughly one-quarter of Ghana's population. Over the next seven years Oxfam supported its Ghanaian partners in their efforts to begin a dialogue with the government on increased transparency and public accountability in the oil and gas industry. Many of Ghana's poorest people are smallholder farmers, so Oxfam and its local partners decided to campaign for "Oil for Agriculture" to ensure that a substantial proportion of the oil revenues would be directed toward assisting impoverished farmers. Oxfam supported research reports and public forums at which the use of revenue from the oil industry was discussed and helped its local partners to raise public awareness of the issue and arrange high-level government meetings. Oxfam's campaign also convinced the World Bank and the International Monetary Fund to focus on how Ghana's income from oil will be spent. The campaign achieved initial success when Ghana's budget for 2014 allocated 15 percent of government oil revenues to agriculture, a 23 percent increase over the previous year's allocation. Ghana's budget for 2014 will receive approximately US$777 million in oil revenues, so 15 percent is $116 million, with the vast majority of this money directed at "poverty-focused agriculture." Oxfam's financial contribution to this outcome was $75,000 in grants to its partners and another $50,000 to sustain the next phase of the campaign, which is designed to ensure that the money is well spent.[11] Indirect costs such as staff time and travel to Ghana are not included in this figure, but rounding it up to $200,000 would probably cover those extra costs. What we cannot know, however, is how much of the oil revenues would have gone to agriculture and specifically to poverty-focused agriculture if Oxfam had not been involved. The government might have reached the same desirable outcome without Oxfam's intervention. A more probable scenario is that in the absence of Oxfam's work some oil revenue, but not as much, would have gone to poverty-focused agriculture. Nevertheless, the extremely modest amount that Oxfam spent, in comparison to the amounts of money at stake, means that even if we say, very conservatively, that Oxfam made it only 1 percent more likely that an extra 15 percent of oil revenue would go to help Ghanaians in extreme poverty (that is, that otherwise none of this revenue would have gone to help them), the charity's actions still had an expected value of 1 percent of $116 million, or $1.16 million. For an outlay of $200,000, that indicates a return on investment of 580 percent. Another way of doing the sums would be to ask, What is the probability that Oxfam's campaign increased, by at least $10 million, the amount of oil revenue that would go to the poor? Again, even if we estimate this probability to be only 10 percent, allowing for a 90 percent probability that Oxfam's campaign either made no difference at all or led to a difference of less than $10 million, then Oxfam's expenditure of $200,000 had an expected value of 10 percent of $10 million, or $1 million, and that still shows a return of 500 percent. This return, moreover, is based only on the budget allocation for 2014; if, as expected, oil revenues continue to flow into the budget for several years, and the principle of allocating 15 percent is retained, the multiyear return would be much higher. Admittedly, this assumes that the government does not use the oil money going to agriculture as an excuse for cutting back other spending on agriculture. It also remains to be seen to what extent the programs are effective in benefiting the smallholder farmers whom they are intended to assist. So the verdict is not yet in, but in this particular instance Oxfam has grounds to be optimistic about its advocacy spending.

Another Oxfam advocacy campaign that appears to be benefiting poor people is an international project called "Behind the Brands" that aims to hold the world's ten biggest food and beverage companies up to scrutiny over ethically sensitive issues like the treatment of small-scale farmers, the sustainable use of water and land, climate change, and the exploitation of women. As part of this campaign Oxfam publicized methods of land acquisition by sugar producers supplying some of the big food brands, showing that in order to expand production they have driven poor people off land they have inhabited for generations, albeit without legal documentation of their ownership. In the northeastern Brazilian state of Pernambuco, for example, a group of fishing families had lived since 1914 on islands in the Sirinhaém River estuary. In 1998 the Usina Trapiche sugar refinery petitioned the state to take over the land. The islanders say that the refinery then followed up its petition by destroying their homes and small farms, threatening further violence to those who did not leave. When the fishing families rebuilt their homes, they were burned down. Coca-Cola and PepsiCo use Usina Trapiche sugar in their products, but until Oxfam's campaign they denied responsibility for the conduct of their suppliers. Oxfam asked all of the Big 10 food brands to show ethical leadership by requiring that their suppliers obtain the free, prior, and informed consent of indigenous and local communities before acquiring land. Nestlé was the first to support this principle fully. Then Coca-Cola declared a policy of zero tolerance for landgrabbing by its suppliers and bottlers and committed to disclosing its suppliers of sugar cane, soy, and palm oil, to conducting social, environmental, and human rights assessments, and to engaging with Usina Trapiche regarding the conflict with the people of the Sirinhaém River estuary. In 2014 PepsiCo also accepted the principle of responsibility for its suppliers. Associated British Foods, the largest sugar producer in Africa and another Big 10 food corporation, is now also committed to the same principle.[12] The gains from these policy commitments are more difficult to quantify than in the example of Ghana's oil revenues, but in the long run they too may be very substantial.

Political advocacy is an attractive option because it responds to critics who say that aid treats just the symptoms of global poverty, leaving its causes untouched. Working to change unfair trading practices that disadvantage developing countries is one way in which we can try to address at least some of the causes of poverty. We can, for example, try to reduce the impact of the so-called resource curse, that is, the paradox that in impoverished countries the discovery of natural resources like oil and minerals is likely to leave levels of poverty untouched or even make them worse. This is in part owing to the impact of a large export industry in raising the value of the country's currency, thus making it harder for local manufacturing industries to compete in international markets. Because manufacturing is likely to be more labor-intensive than oil and mining, this can increase unemployment. Another factor, however, is corruption. In many cases in which foreign companies pay billions of dollars for resource rights, much of the money goes into the pockets of government officials, who then put it into secret accounts abroad. Illicit financial flows from resource-rich developing countries are often many times larger than the total amount of aid the countries receive. Angola, for example, had illicit financial flows of $34 billion between 2000 and 2008, about nine times as much as it received in official development assistance during the same period.[13] Obviously the citizens of the nation, to whom the wealth belongs, are missing out on its benefits, but that is not the greatest harm caused by the corruption. The riches awaiting anyone who can seize control of the government increase the chances of a military coup or an armed insurrection, which can turn into a disastrous civil war. For this reason many antipoverty organizations are part of the Extractive Industries Transparency Initiative, working alongside governments and companies to implement an international standard requiring transparency both from the foreign companies concerning what they pay for rights and from the governments of resource-rich countries concerning what they receive and what happens to it. If this initiative can have an impact on corruption resulting from extractive industries, it will be a highly effective use of the funds the antipoverty organizations put into it.

ONE, the campaign and advocacy organization cofounded by Bono, the lead singer of U2, is the largest advocacy-only organization focused on ending extreme poverty. It has about 160 staff and claims to have over 4 million members, whom it calls upon to sign petitions or contact political leaders; it does not ask the members for donations.[14] Instead, ONE's funds come almost entirely from foundation grants. Do the foundations get good value for their money? Sometimes it appears they do. In 2011 ONE campaigned for nations to increase their pledges to the Global Alliance for Vaccines and Immunization (GAVI). In June 2011 pledges to GAVI totaled $4.3 billion, or more than one hundred times ONE's total expenditure of $29 million that year. But how much of the credit for this can ONE rightly claim? If it can claim 1 percent, then whatever portion of its total expenditure ONE spent on the campaign was money well spent. And ONE conducted other campaigns in 2011 as well, including working with like-minded organizations to make the UN Consolidated Appeal for the Horn of Africa one of the best-funded UN appeals for a humanitarian emergency; in addition, it was part of a successful campaign to persuade the European Commission to propose a law requiring transparency in the extractives industry. In the same year, ONE tracked and publicized G8 countries' progress in meeting their financial and aid effectiveness commitments made at the L'Aquila Summit in 2009. On the other hand, 2011 may have been a particularly successful year. In 2012, a year of economic austerity in Europe, ONE's major achievement was to reduce the size of cuts to the aid budgets of European governments. European government aid budgets are typically both larger, as a percentage of gross national income, and better focused on helping the poor than the U.S. aid budget. So reducing the size of the cuts may also have been a good use of ONE's funds.[15]

GiveWell has gone into partnership with Good Ventures, a philanthropic foundation set up by Cari Tuna and her husband, the Internet entrepreneur Dustin Moskovitz, to set up the Open Philanthropy Project with the goal of investigating a much wider range of giving opportunities than GiveWell does when it evaluates and recommends specific charities. The Open Philanthropy Project, unrestrained by the rigorous methodology of GiveWell's charity evaluations, has written overviews of such topics as funding scientific research, reducing global catastrophic risk, and attempting to reform the criminal justice system in the United States. One of these overviews is on advocacy for improved or increased U.S. foreign aid. After mentioning several examples of policy advocacy that may have contributed to a desirable outcome, the overview concluded that further investigation would be needed before one could be confident that the advocacy groups contribute to the achievement of the outcome. The review concluded, though, that if the advocacy organizations do have an impact, then the return on investment "would likely be very large."[16] In other words, we do not, at present, know enough to say whether policy advocacy offers better or worse value for money than direct aid programs.

15

Preventing Human Extinction

Could we suffer the same fate as the dinosaurs? It is now generally accepted that about sixty-five million years ago a large asteroid or
comet collided with Earth, throwing so much dust into the atmo-
sphere that the Earth became too cold for dinosaurs to survive.
According to the U.S. National Aeronautics and Space Administration
(NASA), collisions with very large objects in space occur "on average
once per 100,000 years, or less often."[1] Perhaps next time, if the object is large enough, it will wipe out our own species. NASA's Near
Earth Object Program is already detecting and tracking asteroids
that could pose some risk of a collision with our planet. Should we
also be putting resources into developing the ability to deflect any
objects that appear to be heading for us? What about other risks of
extinction? The risks may be very small, but human extinction
would, most people think, be very bad. If we are interested in doing
the most good or preventing the most harm, then we should not ignore small risks of major catastrophes.

Nick Bostrom, the director of the Future of Humanity Institute
at the University of Oxford, uses the term *existential risk* to mean a
situation in which "an adverse outcome would either annihilate
Earth-originating intelligent life or permanently and drastically cur-
tail its potential."[2] The reason for specifying "Earth-originating intelligent life" is that what matters is the type of life that exists—is it

intelligent? does it have positive experiences? and so on—not its species. There may be intelligent life elsewhere in the universe, but the universe is not like, say, a mountain valley in which, if one herd of deer is killed, other herbivores will soon migrate into the valley and fill the vacant ecological niche. The universe is so vast and so sparsely inhabited with intelligent life that the extinction of intelligent life originating on Earth would not leave a niche likely to be filled anytime soon, and so it is likely to reduce very substantially the number of intelligent beings who would ever live.

What are the major existential risks? and how likely are we to be able to reduce them? Apart from the risk of a large asteroid colliding with our planet, here are some other ways in which we might become extinct:

- *Nuclear war:* Although the danger seems to have receded since the end of the Cold War, the nuclear powers still possess about seventeen thousand nuclear warheads, more than enough to cause the extinction of all large animals on the planet, including us.[3]
- *Pandemic of natural origin:* The present century has already seen the emergence of several deadly new viruses for which there is no cure. Fortunately, none of them have been highly contagious, but that could change.
- *Pandemic caused by bioterrorism:* Viruses could be deliberately engineered to be both deadly and highly contagious.
- *Global warming:* The most likely predictions are that over the next century global warming will cause regional catastrophes, but not human extinction. The big unknown, however, is feedback loops, for example, from the release of methane caused by the thawing of the Siberian permafrost, which might

go so far as to make the planet uninhabitable, if not in the next century, then within the next five hundred years. That kind of time-scale may give us time to colonize another planet, but it is hard to be confident about that.

- *Nanotech accident:* This scenario involves tiny self-replicating robots multiplying until the entire planet is covered in them. It's also known as the "gray goo" scenario. Let's hope it stays in the realm of science fiction.

- *Physics research producing hyperdense "strange matter":* There has been some speculation that the development of devices like the Large Hadron Collider could produce matter so dense that it would attract nearby nuclei until the entire planet becomes a hyperdense sphere about one hundred meters in diameter.

- *Superintelligent unfriendly artificial intelligence:* Some computer scientists believe that at some point during the present century, artificial intelligence will surpass human intelligence and will then be independent of human control. If so, it might be sufficiently hostile to humans to eliminate us.

In some of these scenarios it isn't easy to say how great the risk is. In others we may be able to estimate the risk but not know how to reduce it. I began this chapter with asteroid collision because we do have a rough idea of the odds in this case and of how to reduce them. If, as NASA says, a collision with an extinction-size asteroid is likely to happen "once in every 100,000 years or less often," we can begin by asking what we ought to do if the upper bound is correct and then consider what difference the "or less often" makes. So, starting with the idea that such a collision is likely to happen once in every one hundred thousand years, the chances of it happening in the next century are 1 in 1,000. NASA is, as mentioned, searching for and tracking objects in space that could collide with us, but if it were to discover something big that was on course to hit us, we do not now have the technical capacity to do anything about it. Whether NASA's tracking system would give us enough warning to develop that capacity—for instance, to build a rocket with a nuclear warhead that could intercept the asteroid and deflect it off its course—is not clear. We could, however, begin to develop the capacity now. Let's say that bringing the project to fruition over the next decade would cost $100 billion. If we assume that it will have a useful lifetime of one hundred years, then there is only a 1 in 1,000 chance we will use it. If we don't, we will have wasted $100 billion. For this expenditure to make sense, we have to value preventing human extinction at more than 1,000 × $100 billion, or more than $100 trillion. How should we judge that figure? U.S. government agencies like the Environmental Protection Agency and the Department of Transportation make estimates of the value of a human life to determine how much it is worth spending to prevent a single death. Their current estimates range from $6 million to $9.1 million.[4] If we suppose the collision will occur at the midpoint of the century, 2050, when the world's population is estimated to reach ten billion, a figure of $100 trillion values each human life at only $10,000. On the basis of the U.S. government agencies' estimates, $100 trillion does not cover even the value of the lives of the more than three hundred million U.S. citizens who would be killed. This suggests that if an extinction-size asteroid is likely to collide with us once in every one hundred thousand years, developing the capacity to deflect an asteroid would be extremely good value.

What if we bring back the "or less often" qualification that NASA put on the likely frequency of an extinction-sized asteroid smashing into the Earth and reduce the odds of it happening within the next century from 1:1000 to 1:100,000 (meaning that such a collision happens only once in every ten million years). If we can eliminate even this much smaller risk for $100 billion, that still looks like good value because it is still valuing a human life at the relatively modest sum of $1 million.

So far we have taken account only of the loss of life of humans existing at the time the collision occurs. That is not all that is at stake. It leaves out both the extinction of other species on our planet and the loss of future generations of human beings. For the sake of simplicity, let's focus on the loss of future generations of human beings. How much difference does that make? Derek Parfit raises the question we are now considering by inviting us to compare three possible outcomes for the planet:

1. Peace;
2. A nuclear war that kills 99 percent of the world's existing population;
3. A nuclear war that kills 100 percent.

Parfit comments as follows:

> (2) would be worse than (1), and (3) would be worse than (2). Which is the greater of these two differences? Most people believe that the greater difference is between (1) and (2). I believe that the difference between (2) and (3) is *very much* greater. . . . The Earth will remain habitable for at least another billion years. Civilization began only a few thousand years ago. If we do not destroy mankind, these few thousand years may be only a tiny fraction of the whole of civilized human history. The difference between (2) and (3) may thus be the difference between this tiny fraction and all of the rest

of this history. If we compare this possible history to a day, what has occurred so far is only a fraction of a second.[5]

Bostrom takes a similar view, beginning his discussion by inviting us to "assume that, holding the quality and duration of a life constant, its value does not depend on when it occurs or on whether it already exists or is yet to be brought into existence as a result of future events and choices."[6] This assumption implies that the value lost when an existing person dies is no greater than the value lost when a child is not conceived, if the quality and duration of the lives are the same. In practice, other factors, like the grief caused to the family of the existing person, would affect our overall judgment of how bad it is for someone to die, as compared to a new person not being conceived. Bostrom is discussing only the more abstract question of the value of a life and is not saying that nothing else matters; nevertheless to think like this about the value of a life takes the idea of impartiality discussed in chapter 7 a controversial step further.

If we accept Bostrom's assumption and if we accept, as Parfit and Bostrom clearly do, that life is to be valued positively—either as it already is or as it is likely to become—then the value lost by human extinction would dwarf the deaths of ten billion people who would be killed if extinction occurs in 2050. Bostrom takes up Parfit's statement that the Earth will remain habitable for a billion years and suggests that we could conservatively assume that it can sustain a population of a billion people for that period. That comes to a billion billion (that is, 10^{18} or a quintillion) human life-years. Even this very large number shrinks to almost nothing when compared with the figures that Bostrom arrives at in his book *Superintelligence*, in which he considers the number of planets that we may, in future, be able to colonize and the possibility that we will develop conscious minds that exist in computer operations rather than biological brains. Allowing for conscious computers gets Bostrom to 10^{58} possible mind-lives. To aid our comprehension of so vast a number, Bostrom writes, "If we represent all the happiness experienced during one entire such life with a single teardrop of joy, then the happiness of these souls could fill and refill the Earth's oceans every second, and keep doing so for a hundred billion billion millennia. It is really important that we make sure these truly are tears of joy."[7] It isn't necessary to accept these more speculative scenarios, however, to show that, if we accept Bostrom's assumption about the value of a human life, reducing existential risk dominates calculations of expected utility. Even the more "conservative" figure of 10^{18} life-years is so large that the expected utility of a very modest reduction of the risk of human extinction overwhelms all the other good things we could possibly achieve.

If reducing existential risk is so important, why has it received so little attention? Bostrom offers several reasons. There has never been an existential catastrophe, and so the prospect of one occurring seems far-fetched. It doesn't help that the topic has been, as Bostrom puts it, "besieged by doom-mongers and crackpots." Other reasons for neglect are familiar from discussions of the psychological barriers that militate against people giving more to reduce global poverty: the lack of identifiable victims and the diffusion of responsibility that occurs when no particular individual, agency, or nation is more responsible for dealing with the problem than any other.[8] I have argued that effective altruists tend to be more influenced by reasoning than by emotions and thus are likely to give where they can do the most good, whether or not there is an identifiable victim. Existential risk, however, takes this abstraction a step further because the overwhelming majority of those who will benefit from the reduction of existential risk do not now exist and, if we were to fail to avert the risk, never would exist. This further step, some will say, isn't just a step beyond our emotional capacity for empathy but one to which our reason can also object. It overlooks what is really so tragic about premature death: that it cuts short the lives of specific living persons whose plans and goals are thwarted. If people are never born, they have not formed any plans or set any goals and hence have less to lose. As this line of argument suggests, just how bad the extinction of intelligent life on our planet would be depends crucially on how we value lives that have not yet begun and perhaps never will begin.

The extraordinary implications of the view that every life counts equally, whether it is the life of someone who will exist whatever we do or a life that will exist only if we make certain choices, might make us keen to reject this view. It has, however, been shared by leading utilitarians. Sidgwick, for example, wrote, "It seems clear that, supposing the average happiness enjoyed remains undiminished, Utilitarianism directs us to make the number enjoying it as great as possible."[9] He then went on to ask what utilitarians should do if increasing the number of people reduces the average level of happiness, but not by enough to fully offset the increase that the additional people bring to the total quantity of happiness. His answer was that we should aim for the greatest total quantity of happiness, not the highest average. Bostrom does not, however, need to take a stance on this issue because he thinks it likely that if we can avoid extinction in the next century or two we will develop the means to make life much better than it is today, so both the total and the average will increase.

The alternative to Bostrom's assumption is what I have elsewhere called the prior existence view: that if people or, more broadly, sentient beings, exist or will exist independently of anything we choose to do, we ought to make their lives as good as possible; but we have no obligation to try to bring about the existence of people who, but for our actions, would not have existed at all.[10] This view fits with the common belief that there is no obligation to reproduce, even if one could give one's children a good start in life and they would be likely to live happy lives. It does, however, face powerful objections. Would it be right for us to solve our environmental problems by all agreeing to put a sterilizing agent in the water supply, thereby deciding to become the last generation on Earth? Assume this is really what, on balance, everyone wants, and no one is unhappy about not having children or troubled by the thought of our species becoming extinct. What everyone wants is the kind of luxurious lifestyle that requires burning vast amounts of fossil fuel but without the guilt that would be involved in handing on to future generations a blighted planet. (If you are wondering what will happen to nonhuman animals, assume that we can find a way of sterilizing them all too.) If ending the extraordinary story of intelligent life on Earth benefits existing beings and harms no one, is it ethically acceptable? If not, then the prior existence view cannot be the whole truth about the value of future beings.[11]

In practice, as the example of preventing a possible asteroid collision indicates, the case for reducing at least some of the risks of extinction is extremely strong, whether we do it to preserve the lives of those who already exist or will exist independently of what we do, or for the sake of future generations who will come into existence only if intelligent life continues on this planet. What is at stake in the perplexing philosophical debate about the value of merely possible future generations is the extent of the efforts we should make to reduce the risk of extinction. On the expected utility calculations that follow from even the more conservative of Bostrom's calculations, it seems that reducing existential risk should take priority over doing other good things. Resources are scarce, and in particular altruistic dollars are scarce, so the more effective altruists donate to reducing existential risk, the less they will be able to donate to helping people in extreme poverty or to reducing the suffering of animals. Should the reduction of existential risk really take priority over these other causes? Bostrom is willing to draw this conclusion: "Unrestricted altruism is not so common that we can afford to fritter it away on a plethora of feel-good projects of suboptimal efficacy. If benefiting humanity by increasing existential safety achieves expected good on a scale many orders of magnitude greater than that of alternative contributions, we would do well to focus on this most efficient philanthropy."[12] To refer to donating to help the global poor or reduce animal suffering as a "feel-good project" on which resources are "frittered away" is harsh language. It no doubt reflects Bostrom's frustration that existential risk reduction is not receiving the attention it should have, on the basis of its expected utility. Using such language is nevertheless likely to be counterproductive. We need to encourage more people to be effective altruists, and causes like helping the global poor are more likely to draw people toward thinking and acting as effective altruists than the cause of reducing existential risk. The larger the number of people who are effective altruists, the greater the likelihood that at least some of them will become concerned about reducing existential risk and will provide resources for doing so.

One obstacle to the conclusion that reducing existential risk is the most efficient form of philanthropy is that often we do not have a clear sense of how we can reduce that risk. Bostrom himself has written, "The problem of how to minimize existential risk has no known solution."[13] That isn't true of all existential risks. We know enough about what it would take to prevent a large asteroid from colliding with our planet to begin work on that project. For many other risks, however, we do not. What will it take to stop bioterrorism? Today, scientists working with viruses are in a situation similar to that of scientists working in atomic physics before World War II. Physicists at the time discussed whether they should publish material that could show how to build a bomb far more lethal than any that had previously been possible. Some of this work was published, and German as well as British and American physicists were aware of it. We are fortunate that the Nazis did not succeed in building an atomic bomb. Now, for good or evil, it is no longer possible to put nuclear weapons back in the box. In the life sciences, to give just one of several examples, researchers at the State University of New York at Stony Brook synthesized a live polio virus. They published the results in *Science*, saying that they "made the virus to send a warning that terrorists might be able to make biological weapons without obtaining a natural virus."[14] Did the research and its publication therefore reduce the risk of bioterrorism causing human extinction? Or did it alert potential bioterrorists to the possibility of synthesizing new viruses? How can we know?

Some effective altruists have shown special interest in the dangers inherent in the development of artificial intelligence (AI). They see the problem as one of ensuring that AI will be friendly, by which they mean, friendly to humans. Luke Muehlhauser, the executive director of Machine Intelligence Research Institute, or MIRI, argues that once we develop a form of AI sophisticated enough to start improving itself, a cascade of further improvements will follow, and "at that point, we might as well be dumb chimpanzees watching as those newfangled 'humans' invent fire and farming and writing and science and guns and planes and take over the whole world. And like the chimpanzee, at that point we won't be in a position to negotiate with our superiors. Our future will depend on what *they* want."[15] The analogy is vivid but double-edged. Granted, the evolution of superior intelligence in humans was bad for chimpanzees, but it was good for humans. Whether it was good or bad from (to use Sidgwick's phrase) "the point of view of the universe" is debatable, but if human life is sufficiently positive to offset the suffering we have inflicted on animals and if we can be hopeful that in the future life will get better both for humans and for animals, then perhaps it will turn out to have been good. Remember Bostrom's definition of existential risk, which refers to the annihilation not of human beings but of "Earth-originating intelligent life." The replacement of our species by some other form of conscious intelligent life is not in itself, impartially considered, catastrophic. Even if the intelligent machines kill all existing humans, that would be, as we have seen, a very small part of the loss of value that Parfit and Bostrom believe would be brought about by the extinction of Earth-originating intelligent life. The risk posed by the development of AI, therefore, is not so much whether it is friendly to us, but whether it is friendly to the idea of promoting well-being in general for all sentient beings it encounters, itself included. If there is any validity in the argument presented in chapter 8, that beings with highly developed capacities for reasoning are better able to take an impartial ethical stance, then there is some reason to believe that, even without any special effort on our part, superintelligent beings, whether biological or mechanical, will do the most good they possibly can.

If we have a clear understanding of what we can do to reduce some existential risks but not others, it may be better to focus on reducing those risks about which we do have such an understanding, while spending a modest amount of resources on doing more research into how we might reduce the risks about which we currently lack the necessary understanding.

Another strategy, for those who share Parfit's and Bostrom's view about the supreme importance of ensuring the preservation of at least some intelligent beings on this planet, even if 99 percent of them are annihilated, would be to build a secure, well-stocked refuge designed to protect a few hundred beings from a wide range of catastrophes that might otherwise cause the extinction of our species. The refuge could be kept populated with rotating populations, selected for genetic diversity and screened for infectious diseases before entering.[16] Even so, the refuge could not protect its occupants against all the extinction scenarios mentioned above. Moreover, the existence of such a refuge poses the danger that political leaders may be more willing to take risks with the lives of others if they know they and their families would survive a nuclear war or some other disastrous consequence of a risky policy they may be tempted to implement. That danger could be avoided if national leaders were unable to enter the refuge, but with some of the political systems we have now, it is difficult to see how their entry could be prevented.

In this chapter I have been exploring the further reaches of conversations in which philosophers and some of the more philosophically minded effective altruists engage. If these discussions lead in strange directions, never mind. One common strategy on which we should all be able to agree is to take steps to reduce the risk of human extinction when those steps are also highly effective in benefiting existing sentient beings. For example, eliminating or decreasing the consumption of animal products will benefit animals, reduce greenhouse gas emissions, and lessen the chances of a pandemic resulting from a virus evolving among the animals crowded into today's factory farms, which are an ideal breeding ground for viruses. That therefore looks like a high-priority strategy. Other strategies that offer immediate benefits while reducing existential risk might be educating and empowering women, who tend to be less aggressive than men. Giving them greater say in national and international affairs could therefore reduce the chances of nuclear war. Educating women has also been shown to lead them to have fewer and healthier children, and that will give us a better chance of stabilizing the world's population at a sustainable level.

Afterword

As I complete this book, in August 2014, it would be easy to think of the world as increasingly dominated by people who are indifferent to suffering and ready to kill to further their nationalist or religious goals. The headlines are full of the consequences of actions that are at the opposite end of the moral spectrum from effective altruism. Separatists in Ukraine have taken up arms against the national government, and the resulting conflict has killed hundreds of civilians on the ground as well as nearly three hundred in the air when a passenger plane was destroyed by a missile. The long-running conflict between Israel and Palestinians has again become deadly, with Hamas launching rockets from sites hidden in densely populated areas of Gaza, and Israeli forces inflicting heavy casualties on civilians as well as militants. There is more conflict in Iraq and Afghanistan, and the civil war continues in Syria, with no prospect of a better future for that unfortunate country. No wonder that when I speak about effective altruism I am often asked how I can remain optimistic about human nature and its potential for altruism.

If the world seems to be a more violent and dangerous place than ever before, however, this impression is an artifact of the media. There are plenty of violent people, but for any randomly selected person today the chances of meeting a violent death at the hands of his or her fellow humans is lower now than it has ever been in human history.[1] "Peace Continues in North America" (or in most of Europe or China or India or South America) does not make a good media headline and neither, it seems, does steady progress in reducing human suffering and premature death.

Here is one example of that progress. In 2009, when I wrote *The Life You Can Save*, I drew on the latest UNICEF report on deaths in children, which showed that nearly 10 million children were dying each year from avoidable, poverty-related causes. The next year, when the paperback came out, that figure had dropped to below 9 million. As I complete this book, the most recent UNICEF estimate is 6.3 million. On a daily basis, in five years the number of children dying from preventable diseases has dropped from 27,000 to 17,000. I have no desire to underestimate the tragedy that is happening in Syria, which is the bloodiest of the current conflicts, but even there, the average daily death toll over the past three years has been fewer than 150.[2] If that toll makes us feel that the struggle for a better world is hopeless, the fact that 10,000 fewer children are dying every day— and altruistic efforts to protect these children from malaria, measles, diarrhea, and pneumonia have played a major part in saving their lives—should restore some balance to the picture and encourage us to do more, until large-scale deaths from preventable diseases no longer occur.

In describing the lives of a few effective altruists, I have emphasized what is distinctive about effective altruism and sought to show how the new movement broadens the range of possibilities for ethical living. As a result, I may have left the impression that to be an effective altruist requires making choices that, to most people, seem extreme: donating half of one's income to effective charities, choosing the career that will enable one to earn more in order to be able to give more, donating a kidney to a stranger. In closing, therefore, I should reiterate that the majority of people involved in effective altruism still have both their kidneys, are continuing in the career paths they had or planned to have before they heard of effective altruism, and are more likely to be giving about one-tenth of their income than half of it.

Effective altruism is an advance in ethical behavior as well as in the practical application of our ability to reason. I have described it as an emerging movement, and that term suggests that it will continue to develop and spread. If it does, then once there is a critical mass of effective altruists, it will no longer seem odd for anyone to regard bringing about "the most good I can do" as an important life goal. If effective altruism does become mainstream, I would expect it to spread more rapidly, for then it will be apparent that it is easy to do a great deal of good and feel better about your life as a result. Whether and, if so, when, that critical mass is reached will depend on the readiness of people all over the world to espouse a new ethical ideal: to do the most good they can.

Notes

Chapter 1. What Is Effective Altruism?

1. Emails from Matt Wage to the author, 2013–14, and Matt's visit to my class at Princeton University, October 23, 2013. The class was recorded and is part of "Practical Ethics," first offered on Coursera in March–June 2014.

2. "Effective Altruism," Wikipedia, http://en.wikipedia.org/wiki/Effective_altruism, April 15, 2014.

3. Dean Karlan and Daniel Wood, "The Effect of Effectiveness: Donor Response to Aid Effectiveness in a Direct Mail Fundraising Experiment," Economic Growth Center Discussion Paper No. 1038/Economics Department Working Paper No. 130, Yale University, April 15, 2014, http://ssrn.com/abstract=2421943; see especially pages 2–5 for a discussion of warm-glow giving, and page 15 for the reference to gifts that are less than the processing costs. For other studies of warm-glow giving, see Heidi Crumpler and Philip J. Grossman, "An Experimental Test of Warm Glow Giving," *Journal of Public Economics* 92 (2008): 1011–21; and Clair Null, "Warm Glow, Information, and Inefficient Charitable Giving," *Journal of Public Economics* 95 (2011): 455–65.

4. Make-A-Wish Foundation, "Miles' Wish to Be Batkid," http://sf.wish.org/wishes/wish-stories/i-wish-to-be/wish-to-be-batkid.

5. See, for example, Holden Karnofsky, "Deep Value Judgments & Worldview Characteristics," http://blog.givewell.org/2013/04/04/deep-value-judgments-and-worldview-characteristics.

6. Ibid.

7. The figures for the Princeton and Yale endowments are taken from Daniel Johnson, "Updated: Princeton Endowment Rises 19.6%, Now Valued at $21 Billion," *Daily Princetonian*, October 17, 2014, http://dailyprincetonian.com/news/2014/10/

endowment_rises_to_21_billion/; and Michael MacDonald, "Harvard's 15.4% Gain Trails as Mendillo Successor Sought," *Bloomberg News*, September 24, 2014, http://www.bloomberg.com/news/2014-09-23/harvard-has-15-4-investment-gain-trailing-dartmouth-penn-1-.html.

Chapter 2. A Movement Emerges

1. The essay will be reprinted and published as a book by Oxford University Press, New York, in 2015.

2. Ian Parker, "The Gift," *New Yorker*, August 2, 2004.

3. Esther Duflo, "Social Experiments to Fight Poverty," TED Talk, February 2010, http://www.ted.com/talks/esther_duflo_social_experiments_to_fight_poverty.

4. For more discussion of GiveWell and its methods of assessment, see chapter 14. For GiveWell's impact in moving donations, see http://www.givewell.org/about/impact.

5. Tom Geoghegen, "Why I'm Giving £1m to Charity," *BBC News Magazine*, December 13, 2010, http://www.bbc.co.uk/news/magazine–11950843; email from Toby Ord to the author, July 2014.

6. The fifty thousand years of healthy life comes from http://www.giving-whatwecan.org/about-us/history/profile-of-founder (2/20/14). On other occasions Ord has quoted the figure for preventing blindness.

7. Geoghegen, "Why I'm Giving £1m to Charity"; email from Toby Ord to the author, July 2014. By 2014 inflation had pushed the £18,000 back up to nearly £20,000.

8. http://www.givingwhatwecan.org (October 25, 2014).

9. http://80000hours.org/about-us.

10. William MacAskill, "The History of the Term 'Effective Altruism,'" March 10, 2014, http://www.effective-altruism.com/the-history-of-the-term-effective-altruism/.

11. http://www.thelifeyoucansave.org/AboutUs/ImpactReport.aspx.

Chapter 3. Living Modestly to Give More

1. Julia Wise, "It Doesn't Have to Be Hard," March 11, 2013, http://www.givinggladly.com/2013/03/it-doesnt-have-to-be-hard.html.

2. The budget data and related information were supplied by Julia Wise to the author, July 2014.

3. Quoted from Paul VI, *Populorum Progressio* (1967), paragraph 23.

4. Thomas Aquinas, *Summa Theologica*, II-II, Q66 A 7.

5. Pope Francis, *Fraternity, the Foundation and Pathway to Peace*, available at http://www.vatican.va/holy_father/francesco/messages/peace/documents/papa-francesco_20131208_messaggio-xlvii-giornata-mondiale-pace–2014_en.html.

6. The Gospel According to St. Mark, 10:21, New International Version. For other gospel references indicating the importance of giving to the poor, see Luke 10:33, 14:13, and Matthew 25:31–46.

7. See www.aaronmoore.com.au. The statement is from Peter Singer, *Practical Ethics*, 3d ed. (Cambridge: Cambridge University Press, 2011), 200. A similar statement appears in my "Famine, Affluence and Morality," *Philosophy and Public Affairs* 1 (1972).

8. Kaley Payne, "Christian Artist Sells All He Has and Gives to the Poor," *Eternity Newspaper*, December 4, 2012, http://www.biblesociety.org.au/news/christian-artist-sells-all-he-owns-and-gives-to-the-poor; Aaron Moore, "Reflections of a Man Who Sold Everything He Had and Gave It to the Poor," *Eternity Newspaper*, July 1, 2013, http://www.biblesociety.org.au/news/reflections-of-a-man-who-sold-everything-and-gave-it-to-the-poor.

9. http://www.givinggladly.com/2013/06/cheerfully.html.

10. The quotes are from remarks Julia made during her visit to Princeton University on November 4, 2013. The class was recorded and is part of "Practical Ethics," offered on Coursera in 2014.

11. http://boldergiving.org/stories.php?story=Julia-Wise-and-Jeff-Kaufman_97.

12. http://www.givinggladly.com/2013/11/but-what-will-my-friends-think.html.

13. Tara Cousineau and Alice Domar, "Psychological Impact of Infertility," *Best Practice & Research Clinical Obstetrics & Gynaecology* 21 (2007): 293–308; I owe this reference to Bernadette Young.

14. Bernadette Young, "Parenthood and Effective Altruism," April 13, 2014, http://www.effective-altruism.com/parenthood-and-effective-altruism.

15. http://www.givinggladly.com/2014/03/the-other-mother.html.

16. Rhema takes her ranking from Giving What We Can (http://www.givingwhatwecan.org/why-give/how-rich-am-i).

17. Rhema Hokama has blogged about her giving at http://www.thelifeyoucansave.org/Blog.aspx. Other quotes and details are taken from her emails to the author, March–July 2014.

Chapter 4. Earning to Give

1. I owe the reference to Wesley to Jeff Kaufman, who has discussed the history of the idea of earning to give in three postings: http://www.jefftk.com/p/history-of-earning-to-give; http://www.jefftk.com/p/history-of-earning-to-give-ii; and http://www.jefftk.com/p/history-of-earning-to-give-iii-john-wesley.

2. Associated Press, "Former Telecom Millionaire Giving Fortune to Children's Causes," http://www.ksl.com/?nid=148&sid=88335.

3. http://80000hours.org/earning-to-give; the point about replaceability seems to have been first made by Brian Tomasik, in "Why Activists Should Consider Making Lots of Money" (2006), http://www.utilitarian-essays.com/make-money.html.

4. Emails to the author, January–February 2013 and March–July 2014.

5. See http://reg-charity.org/. Philipp Gruissem provided information in an email to the author, July 24, 2014; see also Lee Davy, "A Life Outside Poker: Philipp Gruissem—An Effective Altruist," February 19, 2014, http://calvinayre.com/2014/02/19/poker/philipp-gruissem-life-outside-of-poker-ld-audio-interview/.

6. Dylan Matthews, "Join Wall St., Save the World," *Washington Post*, May 31, 2013, http://www.washingtonpost.com/blogs/wonkblog/wp/2013/05/31/join-wall-street-save-the-world/.

7. David Brooks, "The Way to Produce a Person," *New York Times*, June 3, 2013, http://www.nytimes.com/2013/06/04/opinion/brooks-the-way-to-produce-a-person.html?_r=2&.

8. The preceding paragraphs are based on emails to the author from the people mentioned, dating between January 2013 and July 2014.

9. Cartoon by P. C. Vey, *New Yorker*, March 31, 2014, 27.

10. Bernard Williams, "A Critique of Utilitarianism," in J. J. C. Smart and Bernard Williams, eds., *Utilitarianism For and Against* (Cambridge: Cambridge University Press, 1973), 97–98.

11. Ibid., 116–17.

12. All of which confirms a comment made by R. M. Hare, pointing out that Williams's objection to utilitarianism is remarkable for "the boldness of the persuasive definition by which he labels the self-centred pursuit of one's own projects 'integrity' and accounts it a fault in utilitarianism that it could conflict with this." R. M. Hare, "Ethical Theory and Utilitarianism," in R. M. Hare, *Essays in Ethical Theory* (Oxford: Clarendon Press, 1989), 219n.

13. Anonymous comment made in a discussion forum about earning to give on Peter Singer's Practical Ethics online course, April 2014.

14. It is possible to value equality for its own sake and still be very supportive of effective altruism. Philosophers who are sympathetic to some form of egalitarianism and also supportive of effective altruism include Nir Eyal, Thomas Pogge, Larry Temkin, and Alex Voorhoeve.

15. See Angus Deaton, *The Great Escape: Health, Wealth, and the Origins of Inequality* (Princeton: Princeton University Press, 2013).

16. David Irving, *The Mare's Nest,* rev. ed. (London: Panther Books, 1985), 259–62.

17. See Brad Hooker, *Ideal Code, Real World* (Oxford: Clarendon Press, 2002), or Hooker's "Rule Consequentialism," in *Stanford Encyclopedia of Philosophy,* Spring 2011 ed., Edward N. Zalta, ed., http://plato.stanford.edu/archives/spr2011/entries/consequentialism-rule.

18. See, for example, Christopher Kutz, *Complicity: Ethics and Law for a Collective Age* (Cambridge: Cambridge University Press, 2000).

19. The preceding discussion was stimulated by a comment made by Shelly Kagan after one of the Castle Lectures.

20. Morley Winograd and Michael Hais, *How Millennials Could Upend Wall Street and Corporate America,* Brookings Institute, Washington, DC, 2014, http://www.brookings.edu/~/media/research/files/papers/2014/05/millennials%20wall%20st/brookings_winogradv5.pdf.

Chapter 5. Other Ethical Careers

1. MacAskill said this in response to a question from Jeff Kaufman: https://www.facebook.com/jefftk/posts/613456690752?comment_id=713258.

2. See, for example, The World Food Prize, "About Dr. Norman Borlaug," http://www.worldfoodprize.org/en/dr_norman_e_borlaug/about_norman_borlaug/.

3. Benjamin Todd, "Which Cause Is Most Effective?," January 21, 2014, http://80000hours.org/blog/300-which-cause-is-most-effective-300.

4. Wojciech Bonowicz and Janina Ochojska, *Niebo to inni* (Krakow: Znak, 2000), 183.

5. Polish Humanitarian Action, *Annual Report, 2012;* http://www.pah.org.pl/m/3626/PAH%20raport%20roczny%202012en.pdf.

6. Tzu Chi, "Biography of Dharma Master Cheng Yen," http://www.tzuchi. org.tw/en/index.php?option=com_content&view=article&id=159&Itemid=198.

7. "Tzu Chi Fundraising for Japan Earthquake and Tsunami Survivors," USA Tzu Chi, March 18, 2011; "International Buddhist Organization Tzu Chi Foundation Giving Sandy Victims $600 Visa Debit Cards," *New York Daily News*, November 18, 2012;http://www.nydailynews.com/new-york/buddhist-organization-sandy-victims–600-debit-cards-article–1.1204224.

8. Paul Niehaus provided information for this section.

9. Peter Singer, "Animal Liberation," *New York Review of Books*, April 5, 1973.

10. For details, see Peter Singer, *Ethics into Action: Henry Spira and the Animal Rights Movement* (Lanham, Md.: Rowman and Littlefield, 1998).

Chapter 6. Giving a Part of Yourself

1. John Arthur, "Rights and the Duty to Bring Aid," in William Aiken and Hugh LaFollette, eds., *World Hunger and Moral Obligation* (Upper Saddle River, N.J.: Prentice-Hall, 1996).

2. Emails from Chris Croy to the author, January 2013, March 2014, and April 2014.

3. Sally Satel, "Why People Don't Donate Their Kidneys," *New York Times*, May 3, 2014; Living Kidney Donors Network, http://www.lkdn.org/kidney_tx_ waiting_list.html.

4. The quotes are from Alexander's remarks via videolink to my class at Princeton University on November 4, 2013. The class was recorded and is part of Practical Ethics, offered on Coursera in 2014; and from Alexander Berger, "Why Selling Kidneys Should Be Legal," *New York Times*, December 5, 2011.

5. T. Bergstrom, R. Garratt, and D. Sheehan-Connor, "One Chance in a Million: Altruism and the Bone Marrow Registry," *American Economic Review* 99 (2009): 1310.

6. M. A. Landolt et al., "Living Anonymous Kidney Donation," *Transplantation* 71 (2001): 1690–96; I owe the reference to Sue Rabbitt Roff, "Self-Interest, Self-Abnegation and Self-Esteem: Towards a New Moral Economy of Non-directed Kidney Donation," *Journal of Medical Ethics* 33 (2007): 437–41.

7. Ian Parker, "The Gift," *New Yorker*, August 2, 2004, 61.

8. U.S. Department of Health and Human Services Organ Procurement and Transplantation Network database, with thanks to Denise Tripp of United Network

for Organ Sharing, who helped me to extract the data. Available at http://optn. transplant.hrsa.gov/latestData/rptData.asp.

9. Sue Roff, "We Really Need to Talk About Altruism," unpublished, no date.

10. "Stranger Kidney Donations Rising," *BBC News*, June 23, 2009, http://news.bbc.co.uk/1/hi/health/8114688.stm.

11. Di Franks, "Altruistic Kidney Donation in the UK," April 3, 2011, http://livingkidneydonation.co.uk/altruistic-kidney-donation-in-the-uk.htm, and "Altruistic Kidney Donation Statistics," March 12, 2014, http://livingkidneydonation.co.uk/author/Diane-2. Additional information was supplied by Paul van den Bosch of Give a Kidney, http://www.giveakidney.org. United Kingdom figures are for the financial year, which runs from April 1 to March 31. United States figures are for the calendar year.

Chapter 7. Is Love All We Need?

1. David Hume, *Treatise of Human Nature*, book 3, part 2, sec. 1.

2. Frans de Waal, *Primates and Philosophers* (Princeton: Princeton University Press, 2006), 53.

3. Sober and Wilson, *Unto Others: The Evolution and Psychology of Unselfish Behavior* (Cambridge: Harvard University Press, 1998), 9.

4. Frans de Waal, *The Age of Empathy* (New York: Crown, 2009), ix.

5. Jeremy Rifkin, *The Empathic Civilization* (New York: Tarcher/Penguin, 2009).

6. Barack Obama, "Commencement Address at Northwestern University," Northwestern News Service, June 22, 2006. I owe the reference to de Waal, *The Age of Empathy*, ix.

7. "Pinay Girl Writes to Obama, Gets Response," http://www.philstar.com/news-feature/413043/pinay-girl-writes-obama-gets-response; I owe the reference to Paul Bloom, "The Baby in the Well: The Case Against Empathy," *New Yorker*, May 20, 2013. For many other examples of both Barack Obama's and Michelle Obama's references to empathy, see http://cultureofempathy.com/Obama/VideoClips.htm.

8. See M. H. Davis, "Measuring Individual Differences in Empathy: Evidence for a Multidimensional Approach," *Journal of Personality and Social Psychology* 44 (1983): 113–26. I owe this reference to Ezequiel Gleichgerrcht and Liane Young, "Low Levels of Empathic Concern Predict Utilitarian Moral Judgment," *PLOS ONE* 8 (2013): e60418.

9. Paul Slovic, David Zionts, Andrew K. Woods, Ryan Goodman, and Derek Jinks, "Psychic Numbing and Mass Atrocity," in Eldar Shafir, ed., *The Behavioral Foundations of Public Policy* (Princeton: Princeton University Press, 2013), 126–42.

10. Tehila Kogut and Ilana Ritov, "The 'Identified Victim' Effect: An Identified Group, or Just a Single Individual?," *Journal of Behavioral Decision Making* 18 (2005): 157–67.

11. Bloom, "The Baby in the Well."

12. Gleichgerrcht and Young, "Low Levels of Empathic Concern," e60418. For an entertaining discussion of trolley problems, see David Edmonds, *Would You Kill the Fat Man? The Trolley Problem and What Your Answer Tells Us about Right and Wrong* (Princeton: Princeton University Press, 2013).

13. C. D. Navarrete, M. M. McDonald, M. L. Mott, and B. Asher, "Virtual Morality: Emotion and Action in a Simulated Three-Dimensional 'Trolley Problem,'" *Emotion* 12 (2011): 364–70. I owe this reference to Gleichgerrcht and Young.

14. Bloom, "The Baby in the Well."

15. Immanuel Kant, *Critique of Practical Reason*, trans. L. W. Beck (New York: Library of Liberal Arts, 1956), 166.

16. *The Methods of Ethics*, 382. The following account of Sidgwick's view of how ethical judgments can be motivating draws on Katarzyna de Lazari-Radek and Peter Singer, *The Point of View of the Universe* (Oxford: Oxford University Press, 2014).

17. *The Methods of Ethics*, 40, 500.

Chapter 8. One Among Many

1. Bernard Williams, "The Point of View of the Universe: Sidgwick and the Ambitions of Ethics," *Cambridge Review*, May 7, 1982, 191; reprinted in Bernard Williams, *The Sense of the Past: Essays in the History of Philosophy*, ed. Myles Burnyeat (Princeton: Princeton University Press, 2006). For a recent defense of a similar view, see Stephen Asma, *Against Unfairness* (Chicago: University of Chicago Press, 2012). Asma acknowledges his indebtedness to Williams on page 183, note 22.

2. For a fuller account, see Katarzyna de Lazari-Radek and Peter Singer, "The Objectivity of Ethics and the Unity of Practical Reason," *Ethics* 123 (2012): 9–31; for critical discussion, see http://peasoup.typepad.com/peasoup/2012/12/ethics-discussions-at-pea-soup-katarzyna-de-lazari-radek-and-peter-singer-the-objectivity-of-ethics–1.html, and Guy Kahane, "Evolution and Impartiality," *Ethics* 124 (2014): 327–41.

3. Rachel Maley, "Choosing to Give," The Life You Can Save blog, April 9, 2014, http://www.thelifeyoucansave.org/blog/tabid/107/id/69/choosing-to-give.aspx.

4. David Brooks, "The Way to Produce a Person," *New York Times*, June 3, 2013.

5. For another example, this time applied as an argument for giving locally rather than internationally, see William Schambra, "The coming showdown between philanthrolocalism and effective altruism," *Philanthropy Daily*, May 22, 2014, http://www.philanthropydaily.com/the-coming-showdown-between-philanthrolocalism-and-effective-altruism/.

6. Dean Karlan and Daniel Wood, "The Effect of Effectiveness: Donor Response to Aid Effectiveness in a Direct Mail Fundraising Experiment," Economic Growth Center Discussion Paper No. 1038/Economics Department Working Paper No. 130, Yale University, April 15, 2014, http://ssrn.com/abstract=2421943, p. 13.

7. See Joshua Greene, *Moral Tribes: Emotion, Reason, and the Gap Between Us and Them* (New York: Penguin, 2013).

8. J. D. Greene, L. E. Nystrom, A. D. Engell, J. W. Darley, and J. D. Cohen, "The Neural Bases of Cognitive Conflict and Control in Moral Judgment," *Neuron* 44 (2004): 389–400.

9. Paul Conway and Bertram Gawronski, "Deontological and Utilitarian Inclinations in Moral Decision Making: A Process Dissociation Approach," *Journal of Personality and Social Psychology* 104 (2013): 216–35; see also J. Greene, S. A. Morelli, K. Lowenberg, L. E. Nystrom, and J. D. Cohen, "Cognitive Load Selectively Interferes with Utilitarian Moral Judgment," *Cognition* 107 (2008): 1144–54.

10. For a summary of the evidence, see Joshua Greene, "Beyond Point-and-Shoot Morality: Why Cognitive (Neuro)Science Matters for Ethics," *Ethics* 124 (2014): 695–726.

11. Holden Karnofsky, "Excited Altruism," GiveWell blog, August 20, 2013, http://blog.givewell.org/2013/08/20/excited-altruism/.

12. See p. 78 above.

13. J. R. Flynn, "The Mean IQ of Americans: Massive Gains 1932 to 1978," *Psychological Bulletin* 95 (1984): 29–51; J. R. Flynn, "Massive IQ Gains in 14 Nations: What IQ Tests Really Measure," *Psychological Bulletin* 101 (1987): 171–91.

14. U. Neisser, "Rising Scores on Intelligence Tests," *American Scientist* 85 (1997): 440–47.

15. James Flynn, *What Is Intelligence? Beyond the Flynn Effect* (Cambridge: Cambridge University Press, 2009).

16. Steven Pinker, *The Better Angels of Our Nature* (New York: Penguin, 2011).

Chapter 9. Altruism and Happiness

1. http://blog.givewell.org/2013/08/20/excited-altruism/.

2. http://www.givingwhatwecan.org/about-us/history/profile-of-founder (2/20/14).

3. Richard Ball and Kateryna Chernova, "Absolute Income, Relative Income, and Happiness," *Social Indicators Research* 88 (2008): 497–529. I owe this reference as well as several others in the following paragraphs to Andreas Mogensen, "Giving Without Sacrifice: The relationship between income, happiness, and giving," http://www.givingwhatwecan.org/sites/givingwhatwecan.org/files/attachments/giving-without-sacrifice.pdf. Anyone interested in a full discussion of this topic will benefit, as I have in writing this section, from Mogensen's excellent summary of the relevant evidence.

4. Lara Aknin, Michael Norton, and Elizabeth Dunn, "From wealth to well-being? Money matters, but less than people think," *Journal of Positive Psychology* 4 (2009): 523–27; Daniel Kahneman, Alan Krueger, David Schkade, Norbert Schwarz, and Arthur Stone, "Would You Be Happier If You Were Richer? A Focusing Illusion," *Science* 312 (2006): 1908–10.

5. Jeanne Arnold, Anthony Graesch, Enzo Raggazini, and Elinor Ochs, *Life at Home in the 21st Century: 32 Families Open Their Doors* (Los Angeles: Cotsen Institute of Archaeology Press, 2012).

6. Graham Hill, "Living with Less, A Lot Less," *New York Times*, March 9, 2013.

7. Ibid.

8. Elizabeth Dunn, Lara Aknin, and Michael Norton, "Spending Money on Others Promotes Happiness," *Science* 319 (2008): 1687–88.

9. Lara Aknin, Christopher Barrington-Leigh, Elizabeth Dunn, et al., "Prosocial Spending and Well-Being: Cross-Cultural Evidence for a Psychological Universal," National Bureau of Economic Research Working Paper 16415, Cambridge, Mass., 2010.

10. A. M. Isen, "Success, Failure, Attention and Reaction to Others: The Warm Glow of Success," *Journal of Personality and Social Psychology* 15 (1970): 294–301;

A. M. Isen and P. F. Levin, "Effect of Feeling Good on Helping: Cookies and Kindness," *Journal of Personality and Social Psychology* 21 (1972): 384–88.

11. Lara Aknin, Elizabeth Dunn, and Michael Norton, "Happiness Runs in a Circular Motion: Evidence for a Positive Feedback Loop between Prosocial Spending and Happiness," *Journal of Happiness Studies* 13 (2012): 347–55.

12. M. D. Jendrisak et al., "Altruistic Living Donors: Evaluation for Nondirected Kidney and Liver Donation," *American Journal of Transplantation* 6 (2006): 115–20. Presumably the willingness to do it again was hypothetical, at least for the kidney donors.

13. Sue Rabbitt Roff, "Self-Interest, Self-Abnegation and Self-Esteem: Towards a New Moral Economy of Non-directed Kidney Donation," *Journal of Medical Ethics* 33 (2007): 437–41.

14. See, for example, M. Garcia, L. Andrade, and M. Carvalho, "Living Kidney Donors—A Prospective Study of Life Before and After Donation," *Clinical Transplantation* 27 (2013): 9–14.

15. Roy Baumeister, Jennifer Campbell, Joachim Krueger, and Kathleen Vohs, "Does High Self-Esteem Cause Better Performance, Interpersonal Success, Happiness, or Healthier Lifestyles?," *Psychological Science in the Public Interest* 4:1 (2003): 1–44; Helen Cheng and Adrian Furnham, "Personality, Self-Esteem, and Demographic Predictions of Happiness and Depression," *Personality and Individual Differences* 34:6 (2003): 921–42.

16. Richard Keshen, *Reasonable Self-Esteem* (Montreal: McGill-Queens University Press, 1996), 7.

17. T. M. Scanlon, *What We Owe to Each Other* (Cambridge: Harvard University Press, 1998).

18. Peter Singer, *Ethics into Action: Henry Spira and the Animal Rights Movement* (Lanham, Md.: Rowman and Littlefield, 1998), 197.

19. For discussion, see Shih Chao-hwieh, *Buddhist Normative Ethics* (Taoyuan, Taiwan: Dharma-Dhatu Publication, 2014), 98–110.

Chapter 10. Domestic or Global?

1. Rockefeller Philanthropy Advisors, *Finding Your Focus in Philanthropy*, http://www.rockpa.org/document.doc?id=165, last visited May 2, 2014.

2. Centers for Disease Control and Prevention, "Eliminating Measles, Rubella, and Congenital Rubella Syndrome (CRS) Worldwide," http://www.cdc.gov/globalhealth/measles/, last updated January 27, 2014.

3. This is said to be the cost over the entire program. Even if it is accurate, this would not mean either that the cost of vaccinating the remaining 16 percent of the world's children would be as low or that it will save lives at the same cost. It is likely that the low-hanging fruit has already been picked, and the costs of reaching the remaining children will be higher, or their risk of contracting measles will be lower, which will also mean that the cost per death averted is higher.

4. http://money.cnn.com/gallery/real_estate/2012/08/20/best-places-top-earning-towns.moneymag/3.html.

5. Jonathan Muraskas and Kayhan Parsi, "The Cost of Saving the Tiniest Lives: NICUs Versus Prevention," *Virtual Mentor* 10 (2008): 655–58, http://virtualmentor.ama-assn.org/2008/10/pfor1–0810.html.

6. Admittedly, almost any claim in ethics has been denied by someone. In this case, it is John Taurek, in "Should the Numbers Count?," *Philosophy and Public Affairs* 6 (1977): 293–316; but Derek Parfit, "Innumerate Ethics," *Philosophy and Public Affairs* 7 (1978): 285–301, shows that Taurek's argument is untenable.

7. I owe this comparison to Toby Ord, "The Moral Imperative Towards Cost-Effectiveness," http://www.givingwhatwecan.org/sites/givingwhatwecan.org/files/attachments/moral_imperative.pdf. Ord suggests a figure of $20 for preventing blindness; I have been more conservative. Ord explains his estimate of the cost of providing a guide dog as follows: "Guide Dogs of America estimate $19,000 for the training of the dog. When the cost of training the recipient to use the dog is included, the cost doubles to $38,000. Other guide dog providers give similar estimates, for example Seeing Eye estimates a total of $50,000 per person/dog partnership, while Guiding Eyes for the Blind estimates a total of $40,000." His figure for the cost of preventing blindness by treating trachoma comes from Joseph Cook et al., "Loss of Vision and Hearing," in Dean Jamison et al., eds., *Disease Control Priorities in Developing Countries*, 2d ed. (Oxford: Oxford University Press, 2006), 954. The figure Cook et al. give is $7.14 per surgery, with a 77 percent cure rate. I thank Brian Doolan of the Fred Hollows Foundation for discussion of his organization's claim that it can restore sight for $25. GiveWell suggests a figure of $100 for surgeries that prevent one to thirty years of blindness and another one to thirty years of low vision but cautions that the sources of these figures are not clear enough to justify a high level of confidence.

8. Office of the Assistant Secretary for Planning and Evaluation, "2014 Poverty Guidelines," http://aspe.hhs.gov/poverty/14poverty.cfm.

9. The figure was calculated by http://www.in2013dollars.com/, using the Consumer Price Index of the U.S. Bureau of Labor Statistics.

10. http://www.fns.usda.gov/pd/supplemental-nutrition-assistance-program-snap; go to "Monthly Data—National Level: FY 2011 Through Latest Available Month."

11. United States Department of Agriculture, Economic Research Service, *Food Security in the U.S.*, http://www.ers.usda.gov/topics/food-nutrition-assistance/food-security-in-the-us.aspx#.U2eAh_mSySo.

12. See Holden Karnofsky, "Hunger Here v Hunger There," November 26, 2009, http://blog.givewell.org/2009/11/26/hunger-here-vs-hunger-there/.

13. For GiveWell's assessment of the benefits gained by cash transfers, see "Cash Transfers in the Developing World," http://www.givewell.org/international/technical/programs/cash-transfers.

14. http://robertwiblin.com/2012/04/06/the-principle-of-altruistic-arbitrage/#comment–1450.

Chapter 11. Are Some Causes Objectively Better than Others?

1. *New York Review of Books*, April 5, 1973.

2. Thomas Scanlon, *What We Owe to Each Other* (Cambridge: Harvard University Press, 1998), 230, 235.

3. Such suspicions can be defended philosophically. For a response to Scanlon on this issue, see Derek Parfit, *On What Matters* (Oxford: Oxford University Press, 2011), 2:193–212.

4. Thanks to Shelly Kagan for suggesting we could consider periods of temporary blindness rather than the risk of blindness.

5. On the Metropolitan Museum of Art: Robin Pogrebin, "In the Met's Future, a Redesigned Modern Art Wing," *New York Times*, May 19, 2014; Metropolitan Museum of Art, "Modern Art: Lila Acheson Wallace Wing," http://www.metmuseum.org/about-the-museum/press-room/general-information/2005/modern-artbrlila-acheson-wallace-wing, and "Metropolitan Museum Reaches One Million Visitors in 18 Months to New Galleries for American Paintings, Sculpture, and Decorative Arts," http://www.metmuseum.org/about-the-museum/press-room/news/2013/american-wing-one-million-visitors. On MoMA: Carol Vogel, "MoMA to Gain Exhibition Space by Selling Adjacent Lot for $125 Million," *New York Times*, January 3, 2007; Museum of Modern Art, Inside Out, June 28, 2011,

https://www.moma.org/explore/inside_out/2011/06/28/counting-down-to-the-years-end-in-june.

6. Melissa Berman, "In Charitable Giving, No 'Hierarchy of Goodness,'" Letter to the Editor, *New York Times*, August 19, 2014.

7. On Aaron Moore, see chap. 3.

8. "An Auctioneer Comes Back to the Business," *New York Times*, April 10, 2014.

9. From an interview with Giancarlo Politi and Helena Kontova, *Flash Art* 132 (1987), available at http://www.flashartonline.com/interno.php?pagina=articolo_det&id_art=348&det=ok&title=JEFF-KOONS.

10. Carol Vogel, "Asian Collectors Give Christie's a High-Yield Night," *New York Times*, May 14, 2014.

11. See p. 56 above.

12. http://www.nrafff.com/ways-of-giving/tax-deductible-gifts.aspx, visited May 7, 2014.

Chapter 12. Difficult Comparisons

1. J. Salomon, T. Vos, D. Hogan, et al., "Common Values in Assessing Health Outcomes from Disease and Injury: Disability Weights Measurement Study for the Global Burden of Disease Study 2010," *Lancet* 380 (2012): 2129–43.

2. For criticism of the discount for blindness, see H. Taylor, J. Jonas, J. Keefe, et al., "Disability Weights for Vision Disorders in Global Burden of Disease Study," *Lancet* 381 (2013): 23; J. Salomon, T. Vos, and C. Murray reply in the same issue, pages 23–24. For discussion of the broader question of the methods used to reach such figures, see John McKie, Jeff Richardson, Peter Singer, and Helga Kuhse, *The Allocation of Health Care Resources: An Ethical Evaluation of the "QALY" Approach* (Aldershot, U.K.: Ashgate Publishing, 1998).

3. For research casting doubt on our judgments even of recent painful or uncomfortable experiences, see Donald Redelmeier and Daniel Kahneman, "Patients' Memories of Painful Medical Treatments: Real-time and Retrospective Evaluations of Two Minimally Invasive Procedures," *Pain* 66:1 (1996): 3–8, and Donald Redelmeier, Joel Katz, and Daniel Kahneman, "Memories of Colonoscopy: A Randomized Trial," *Pain* 104 (2003): 187–94.

4. Holden Karnofsky, "Significant Life Change," GiveWell blog, July 28, 2008, http://blog.givewell.org/2008/07/28/significant-life-change/.

5. Holden Karnofsky, "DALYs and Disagreement," GiveWell blog, August 22, 2008, http://blog.givewell.org/2008/08/22/dalys-and-disagreement/.

6. Toby Ord, "Comment" (August 12, 2008) on Holden Karnofsky, "Disability-Adjusted Life Years II—Variations, August 11, 2008, http://blog.givewell. org/2008/08/11/disability-adjusted-life-years-ii-variations/.

7. John Henry Newman, *Certain Difficulties Felt by Anglicans in Catholic Teaching* (1850; reprint, London: Longmans, Green, 1901), vol. 1, lecture 8, p. 240, available at http://www.newmanreader.org/Works/anglicans/volume1/index.html. For discussion, see Roger Crisp, "Turning Cardinal Newman on His Head: Just How Bad Is a Bad Intention?," University of Oxford Practical Ethics blog, May 22, 2012, http://blog.practicalethics.ox.ac.uk/2012/05/turning-cardinal-newman-on-his-head-just-how-bad-is-a-bad-intention/.

Chapter 13. Reducing Animal Suffering and Protecting Nature

1. See, for example, the Wikipedia page "Animal Rescue Group," http://en.wikipedia.org/wiki/Animal_rescue_group, which is about such organizations.

2. Humane Society of the United States, "Pets by the Numbers," January 30, 2014, http://www.humanesociety.org/issues/pet_overpopulation/facts/pet_owner-ship_statistics.html.

3. Humane Society of the United States, "Farm Animal Statistics: Slaughter Totals," April 17, 2014, http://www.humanesociety.org/news/resources/research/stats_slaughter_totals.html#.U27ZyvmSySo. The figures come originally from the U.S. Department of Agriculture National Agricultural Statistics Service.

4. Matt Ball and Bruce Friedrich, *The Animal Activists' Handbook* (New York: Lantern Books, 2009), 15–16.

5. Harish Sethu, "Is Vegan Outreach Right About How Many Animals Suffer to Death?," http://www.countinganimals.com/is-vegan-outreach-right-about-how-many-animals-suffer-to-death/.

6. Animal Charity Evaluators, FAQ, Position Statement. See http://www.animalcharityevaluators.org/about/faq/ and http://www.animalcharityevaluators.org/about/position-statement/.

7. Peter Singer, *Animal Liberation* (1975; reprint, New York: Harper, 2009), chap. 1; for support for my claim that at a philosophical level the argument against speciesism is "won," see Colin McGinn, "Eating Animals Is Wrong," *London Review of Books*, January 24, 1991, 14–15.

8. See, for example, Carl Cohen, "The Case for the Use of Animals in Biomedical Research," *New England Journal of Medicine* 315 (1986): 865–70; Michael Leahy, *Against Liberation: Putting Animals in Perspective* (London: Routledge, 1991).

9. Henry Sidgwick makes a similar point when responding to the charge that utilitarianism, by including the sufferings of animals in its calculations, greatly increases the difficulties of calculating what will maximize utility. He acknowledges the problem but adds, "Still, the difficulty is at least not greater for Utilitarians than it is for any other moralists who recoil from the paradox of disregarding altogether the pleasures and pains of brutes." *The Methods of Ethics*, 7th ed. (London: Macmillan, 1907), 414.

10. As I have argued in *Practical Ethics*, 3d ed. (Cambridge: Cambridge University Press, 2011), chaps. 4, 5. Note, however, that since writing that I have become more sympathetic to hedonism rather than preference utilitarianism. See Katarzyna de Lazari-Radek and Peter Singer, *The Point of View of the Universe* (Oxford: Oxford University Press, 2014), chaps. 8, 9. For other views on the killing of animals, see Jeff McMahan, "Eating Animals the Nice Way," *Daedalus* (Winter 2008): 66–76, and Tatjana Visak, *Killing Happy Animals* (London: Palgrave Macmillan, 2013).

11. See Animal Charity Evaluators, Leafleting Impact Spreadsheet: http://www.animalcharityevaluators.org/research/interventions/leafleting/leafleting-calculator/ and Online Ads Spreadsheet: http://www.animalcharityevaluators.org/research/interventions/online-ads/online-ads-calculator/.

12. Ben West, "Top Animal Charities and Climate Change," October 14, 2012, http://www.animalcharityevaluators.org/blog/top-animal-charities-and-climate-change. West's case rests on the claim that online ads can lead people to become vegetarian at a cost of $11 per year of vegetarian eating. West based his figure on an estimate of how long people remain vegetarians, a figure that has since been amended to reflect better data. Hence Animal Charity Evaluators now has a "best guess" cost for online ads of $1.46 per vegetarian year, with a range of $0.36–$4.27. The best guess for leafleting is $1.77, with a range of $0.34–$9.02. In other words, the figures are even more favorable to West's conclusion than the one he used. (For details, see the spreadsheets referenced in the previous note; to calculate vegetarian years per dollar, divide 100 by the product of the estimate of "product limiters" and the number of years per limiter.) More studies intended to strengthen the evidential base of these figures are currently under way.

13. Dale Jamieson, *Reason in a Dark Time: Why the Struggle Against Climate Change Failed—and What It Means for Our Future* (Oxford: Oxford University Press, 2014). GiveWell has reviewed geoengineering as an opportunity for effective philanthropy: http://www.givewell.org/labs/causes/geoengineering. Clive Hamilton expresses concerns in *Earthmasters: The Dawn of the Age of Climate Engineering* (New Haven: Yale University Press, 2013).

14. Aldo Leopold, "The Land Ethic," in his *A Sand County Almanac* (New York: Oxford University Press, 1949).

15. Oscar Horta, "Disvalue in Nature and Intervention," *Pensata Animal* 34 (2010), available at https://www.academia.edu/1277396/Disvalue_in_Nature_and_Intervention. See also the essays by Brian Tomasik at http://www.utilitarian-essays.com under the heading "Wild-animal suffering."

16. Singer, *Practical Ethics*, chap. 10; see Lazari-Radek and Singer, *The Point of View of the Universe*, chaps. 8, 9.

Chapter 14. Choosing the Best Organization

1. Bob Ottenhoff and Greg Ulrich, *More Money for More Good* (Washington, D.C.: Guidestar, 2012), 13, available at http://www.guidestar.org/rxg/give-to-charity/money-for-good/index.aspx.

2. See chap. 8.

3. Ottenhoff and Ulrich, *More Money for More Good*, 13.

4. http://www.charitynavigator.org/index.cfm?bay=content.view&cpid=1193#.U37kt_mSySo and http://www.charitynavigator.org/index.cfm?bay=content.view&cpid=483#43.

5. http://blog.givewell.org/2009/12/01/the-worst-way-to-pick-a-charity/.

6. http://www.charitynavigator.org/index.cfm?bay=content.view&cpid=483#43.

7. For an example of the challenge of determining, without proper randomized controlled trials, whether improvements in health and well-being are the result of a specific intervention or of something that is happening on a broader scale, see Michael Clemens and Gabriel Demombynes, "When Does Rigorous Impact Evaluation Make a Difference? The Case of the Millennium Villages," Center for Global Development, Working Paper 225, October 2010, http://www.cgdev.org/publication/when-does-rigorous-impact-evaluation-make-difference-case-millennium-villages-working.

8. Rachel Glennerster, "Improving Primary Education with Evidence," From Evidence to Policy: Decision Science Symposium, Kigali, Rwanda, May 21–23, 2013, availableat:http://www.povertyactionlab.org/doc/rwanda-education-evidence-rachel-glennerster-may–21–2013.

9. "I Was Just Trying to Help," *This American Life*, August 16, 2013, http://www.thisamericanlife.org/radio-archives/episode/503/transcript.

10. Innovations for Poverty Action, "Evaluating the Savings for Change Program in Mali," http://www.poverty-action.org/project/0054.

11. Ghana's expected oil revenue for 2014 is taken from Ministry of Finance, Republic of Ghana, *2014 Citizens Budget*, Accra, 2013, p. 16, available at http://www.mofep.gov.gh/sites/default/files/news/2014_Citizens_Budget_Chapter_3.pdf. Thanks to Oxfam America for their assistance.

12. Oxfam International, *Sugar Rush*, October 2, 2013, http://www.oxfam.org/sites/www.oxfam.org/files/bn-sugar-rush-land-supply-chains-food-beverage-companies–021013-en_1.pdf; Oxfam International, "PepsiCo Declares 'Zero Tolerance' for Land Grabs in Supply Chain," March 18, 2014, http://www.oxfam.org/en/grow/pressroom/pressrelease/2014–03–18/pepsico-declares-zero-tolerance-land-grabs-supply-chain.

13. Organization for Economic Cooperation and Development, DAC International Network on Conflict and Fragility, *Fragile States 2013: Resource Flows and Trends in a Shifting World*, http://www.oecd.org/dac/incaf/FragileStates2013.pdf, pp. 78–79.

14. "About ONE," http://www.one.org/international/about/; GiveWell, "Advocacy for Improved or Increased U.S. Foreign Aid," January 2014, http://www.givewell.org/labs/causes/advocacy-foreign-aid; GiveWell, "A Conversation with Ben Leo," http://files.givewell.org/files/conversations/Ben%20Leo%209–3–13%20(public).pdf.

15. *ONE Annual Report*, 2011, and *ONE Annual Report*, 2012, www.one.org/international/annualreport/.

16. GiveWell, "Advocacy for Improved or Increased U.S. Foreign Aid," January 2014, http://www.givewell.org/labs/causes/advocacy-foreign-aid.

Chapter 15. Preventing Human Extinction

1. National Aeronautics and Space Administration, Near Earth Object Program, Torino Hazard Scale, http://neo.jpl.nasa.gov/torino_scale.html.

2. Nick Bostrom, "Existential Risks: Analyzing Human Extinction Scenarios And Related Hazards," *Journal of Evolution and Technology* 9 (2002), available at www.jetpress.org/volume9/risks.html.

3. Hans Kristensen and Robert Norris, "Global Nuclear Weapons Inventories, 1945–2013," *Bulletin of the Atomic Scientists* 69 (2013): 75–81.

4. Binyamin Appelbaum, "As U.S. Agencies Put More Value on a Life, Businesses Fret," *New York Times*, February 16, 2011.

5. Derek Parfit, *Reasons and Persons* (Oxford: Clarendon Press, 1984), 453–54.

6. Nick Bostrom, "Existential Risk Prevention as Global Priority," *Global Policy* 4 (2013): 16.

7. Nick Bostrom, *Superintelligence: Paths, Dangers, Strategies* (Oxford: Oxford University Press, 2014), 103; see also Bostrom, "Existential Risk Prevention as Global Priority," 18–19. Nick Beckstead argues for a similar position in "The Overwhelming Importance of Shaping the Far Future" (PhD diss., Rutgers University, 2013).

8. Nick Bostrom, Existential Risk FAQ, version 1.2 (2013), no. 9, http://www.existential-risk.org/faq.html.

9. Henry Sidgwick, *The Methods of Ethics*, 7th ed. (London: Macmillan, 1907), 415.

10. See Peter Singer, *Practical Ethics*, 3d ed. (Cambridge: Cambridge University Press, 2011), 88–90, 107–19; for a more recent account of my views on this topic that is fuller than I can present here, see Katarzyna de Lazari-Radek and Peter Singer, *The Point of View of the Universe* (Oxford: Oxford University Press, 2014), 361–77.

11. The most influential critique of views that give priority to those who exist or will exist independently of our decisions is Parfit, *Reasons and Persons*, part 4. For a recent discussion of related views in the context of existential risk, see Beckstead, "The Overwhelming Importance of Shaping the Far Future," chaps. 4, 5.

12. Bostrom, "Existential Risk Prevention as Global Priority," 19.

13. Ibid., 26.

14. A. Pollack, "Scientists Create a Live Polio Virus," *New York Times*, July 2, 2002. I owe this reference and other points in this paragraph to Michael Selgelid, "Governance of Dual-Use Research: An Ethical Dilemma," *Bulletin of the World Health Organization* 87 (2009): 720–23.

15. Luke Muehlhauser, *Facing the Intelligence Explosion*, chap. 13, available at: intelligenceexplosion.com/2012/intelligence-explosion.

16. Nick Bostrom makes such a proposal at http://www.existential-risk.org/faq. html#10.

Afterword

1. Steven Pinker, *The Better Angels of Our Nature* (New York: Viking, 2011).

2. For estimates of the death toll in the Syrian civil war, see http://en.wikipedia. org/wiki/Casualties_of_the_Syrian_Civil_War. At the time of writing the highest of these estimates is 171,509 for a period of a little over three years, which gives a daily average of 144 deaths.

Index

Parts of this book were given as the Castle Lectures in Yale's Program in Ethics, Politics, and Economics, delivered by Peter Singer at Yale University in 2013.

The Castle Lectures were endowed by Mr. John K. Castle. They honor his ancestor the Reverend James Pierpont, one of Yale's original founders. Given by established public figures, Castle Lectures are intended to promote reflection on the moral foundations of society and government and to enhance understanding of ethical issues facing individuals in our complex modern society.